The Lakeland Peaks

Books on Lakeland by the same author

LAKELAND THROUGH THE LENS

LAKELAND JOURNEY

LAKELAND HOLIDAY

OVER LAKELAND FELLS

LAKELAND SCRAPBOOK

ESCAPE TO THE HILLS—PART ONLY

CLIMBING WITH A CAMERA

Companions to this volume

THE WELSH PEAKS

THE SCOTTISH PEAKS

THE PEAK AND PENNINES

Plate 1 Striding Edge—Helvellyn

W. A. Poucher, Hon. F.R.P.S.

The Lakeland Peaks

A Pictorial Guide to walking in the district
and to the safe ascent of its principal mountain groups

with 250 photographs by the author
14 Maps and 141 Routes

Ninth Edition

Constable London

First published in Great Britain 1960
by Constable and Company Ltd
10 Orange Street London WC2H 7EG
Copyright © 1960 by William Arthur Poucher
Second edition 1962
Third edition 1965
Fourth edition 1968
Fifth edition 1971
Sixth edition 1976
Seventh edition 1979
Eighth edition 1981
Ninth edition 1983
ISBN 0 09 465450 6

Set in Monophoto Times New Roman 9pt
Filmset and printed in Great Britain by
BAS Printers Limited, Over Wallop, Hampshire

The author is a member of
The Climbers' Club
The Fell and Rock Climbing Club

Preface to the ninth edition

In this edition I have amended Routes 117 and 121 and in the latter would draw attention to the slippery rocks that deck the near approach to the bridge in Oxendale; great care is essential here and especially so with elderly fell walkers. There is one place where the narrow track leads to a waterfall, with sheer drops on the L to the stream. It would be safer to make the approach higher up the hillside and then descend to the path near the bridge.

Erosion of the paths to the Lakeland Peaks is increasing year by year and is now so serious that it is causing considerable concern in this National Park. The tracks ascending the Langdale Pikes are possibly the most affected in the whole district, and while the weather contributes its quota there is little doubt that the main cause is over-usage by the legions of visitors who tread them. Thus, the Fell Walker is largely responsible for the erosion of Route 104 to Harrison Stickle and of Route 117 to Bow Fell, and it would help if all pedestrians keep off the eroded paths and walk beside them. In the meantime, however, the lower section of Route 104 has been fenced off and a new path made which joins the original one in its higher reaches. But the most serious problem was that of the Raven Crag Screes behind the Old Dungeon Ghyll Hotel which was the special preserve of the Rock Climber on his way to Gimmer Crag, Middlefell Buttress and Raven Crag. This area is the property of the National Trust which has re-routed both ascent and scree-run descent, ably assisted by the BMC and local wardens. The original tracks have been fenced off and a new one made well to the L.

However, on my last visit to Langdale I found the recently improved Route 104 was already showing signs of erosion, as can be seen in Plate 188. and while taking a few photographs I was passed by a continuous stream of walkers of all ages. One group consisted of 45 teenagers from Liverpool who said they had come to the Lakes for just one climb on the first sunny day of June.

There would seem to be no remedy for the prevention of erosion in our most popular National Park, but some years ago I noticed in Western America that it had been retarded by placing tarmac on the most worn parts of some of the trails.

A question that is frequently posed to me is "What cameras do you use?" Well, there is no reason why I should not divulge this seeming secret in print, so I will say that since the availability of 35 mm film I have always used Leicas, and replaced them as new models appeared. I have now two M2s (one of them in case of accident) with 35 mm wide angle, 50 mm normal and 90 mm long focus lenses. These I use for monochrome and my favourite film is Kodak Plus X. I have also a Leicaflex, with 28 mm wide angle, 50 mm normal, 90 mm long focus, 45/90 mm zoom and 135 mm telephoto lenses. I use them exclusively for colour and my favourite film is Kodachrome 25.

In view of the vast scope of this book it is obviously impossible to check frequently every one of the descriptions of the routes. Time, usage, rock falls and local weather may be responsible for slight variations, and should any reader encounter any inaccuracy I would appreciate a note of it for inclusion in future editions of this work.

It should be noted that the Routes described and illustrated herein have been frequented over the years without objection, but they do not necessarily constitute a Right of Way. Should a reader have any doubts, he would be well advised to consult the owner of the land and ask permission to cross it before embarking upon his walk.

In view of the increasing scourge of vandalism that is sweeping the country, and is not unknown in mountainous districts, this advice is of paramount importance because wanton damage to fences, hedges and walls, as well as to summit cairns and shelters, may induce the owners of the land to prohibit access.

Finally, I would urge Leaders of school and youth parties not to venture on these hills unless the weather is favourable, and moreover, they should insist upon everyone wearing boots and proper clothing. For, by doing so, they will not only reduce the risk of accidents but also avoid the often needless call for Mountain Rescue.

A Route Card will be found at the end of this book and is already in use in Scotland and Snowdonia. This should be completed by all climbers and fell walkers as it would be invaluable in the event of an accident by facilitating Mountain Rescue.

However, the Lake District Mountain Accidents Association state that after trial periods of use of cards and route books it was found that any system of this nature was a failure due to people:

1. failing to complete route cards properly and—
2. routes being amended without notification to the establishment where the original route had been left.

The fourteen maps are reproduced with the permission of John Bartholomew & Son Limited.

W A POUCHER
4 Heathfield
Reigate Heath Surrey

Contents

Frontispiece. Striding Edge—Helvellyn   2

Preface   5

Introductory notes   10

Equipment   13
Boots, nailing, clothes, rucksacks, maps,
compass, aneroid, ice axe

Rock climbing   21

The Lakeland centres   22
Wasdale, Ennerdale, Buttermere, Newlands,
Keswick, Borrowdale, Patterdale, Mardale,
Long Sleddale, Kentmere and Troutbeck,
Ambleside and Grasmere, Langdale, Coniston,
Dunnerdale, Eskdale

The Lakeland Peaks   26
Group System for 141 routes of ascent

Heights of the Peaks   32
116 tops arranged according to altitude

Heights of the Passes   34
23 passes arranged according to altitude

Heights above O.D. of the lakes and tarns   35
69 sheets of water arranged according to their
heights above sea level

Mountain photography   37
13 essentials for good mountain pictures and
5 photographs

Photography in the different groups   50
The best pictorial views *of* the groups
The most striking views *from* the groups

Contents

Notes on the routes   57
The 14 mountain groups, the routes,
descents, traverses, the panoramas

Distances and times   58
Formula for calculating distances and times
with an example of the Helvellyn Horseshoe,
which includes Routes 74, 75, 84 and 85

Route finding in mist   60

Accident procedure   61

Brocken spectres   61

Glories   61

Detailed directions for 141 routes
The Approach to Wasdale 1 photograph   62
The Scafell Group 17 Routes and 28 photographs   66
The Gable Group 17 Routes and 33 photographs   104
The Pillar Group 12 Routes and 21 photographs   151
The High Stile Group 9 Routes and 14 photographs   181
The Dale Head Group 8 Routes and 13 photographs   204
The Grasmoor Group 5 Routes and 14 photographs   224
Skiddaw and Blencathra 5 Routes and 12 photographs   246
The Helvellyn Group 8 Routes and 12 photographs   265
The Fairfield Group 9 Routes and 9 photographs   286
High Street, North 8 Routes and 13 photographs   302
High Street, South, and Harter Fell 6 Routes and 7   324
   photographs
The Langdale Pikes 11 Routes and 17 photographs   336
The Bowfell Group 13 Routes and 17 photographs   362
The Coniston Group and Harter Fell, Eskdale 13 Routes   388
   and 32 photographs

Route card   433

Index   437

Introductory notes

Lakeland has for many years been one of the most popular holiday centres in Britain because its matchless beauty provides that peaceful change of environment which appeals to people of all ages. When the energetic youth first visits the district, he raises his eyes to the peaks and imagines himself standing by one of the summit cairns, inhaling the invigorating mountain air and scanning the valleys far below, the chain of engirdling hills and the distant glimmering seas. Come what may, he loses no time in setting out to climb one of them, and realises his ambition with that satisfaction which comes only after the ardours of the ascent. It is quite probable that he will make Scafell Pike his first conquest, not only because it is the monarch of our English hills, but also because he believes it will reveal the finest and most comprehensive panorama on account of its altitude. Once he has trodden the summit, he quite naturally speculates upon the merits of the views from the other high peaks in the district, and after talking over the question with his friends he will in all probability continue his exploration by climbing Great Gable, or Helvellyn, or perhaps even the Old Man of Coniston, on his first holiday.

When this youth returns home his thoughts will often revert to these experiences, and especially if he has been captivated by the spirit and mystery of the hills. He will doubtless unfold his map frequently, and by following the routes thereon he will re-live these happy experiences. If he climbed Scafell Pike from Borrowdale, his thoughts will follow that grand walk from the bus in Seatoller through the delightful terminal stretches of the valley to the hamlet of Seathwaite, the tramp along the stony track to Stockley Bridge with the music of the stream in his right ear, the scramble up the shattered slopes to Taylor Gill Force with perhaps an inquisitive glance into the wild ravine enclosing it, the ramble up the more gentle

declivities of the pass to Sty Head with the sombre Tarn on
the left and the impressive crags of the Central Fells visible all
the way. He remembers that welcome halt for a cigarette and
a chat with another enthusiastic climber near the cairn, and
then on again up the steeper track which suddenly disclosed
the glittering waters of Sprinkling Tarn at the foot of the
gullied precipices of Great End. Soon after that the shelter at
Esk Hause came into view in the dip on the horizon, and
when he had reached it the short walk over to the cairn which
revealed another surprise in the Langdale Pikes and the lakes
glimmering away in the distance to the south-east. Then
followed the high-level tramp along the well-cairned track to
Scafell Pike, the traverse of the great boulder-strewn top of
Broad Crag, and after the crossing of the last steep dip in the
route, the exhilaration of standing by the huge cairn on the
roof of England with a whole kingdom spread out at his feet.

The close inspection of the map will suggest to our friend
many other routes to this lofty Belvedere, and curiosity will
induce him to ponder over their respective merits. Would the
Corridor Route have been more interesting? Perhaps it would
have been a greater thrill to have stayed in Wasdale and to
have ascended the mountain by way of Mickledore, or what
about the approaches from Eskdale via Cam Spout? Then
another line of thought will probably develop, for he had seen
a grand array of peaks engirdling the horizon from the Pike
and he will now speculate again upon the merits of the
panoramas from their summits, to realise quite suddenly that
a lifetime is not too long in which to become acquainted with
them all.

The cogitations of our young friend will follow a normal
course and he will do exactly the same as the rest of us did in
our novitiate, for he will formulate the plans for his next
vacation long before it is due. Next time, he decides, he will
stay in another valley and explore the adjacent hills; but
which one, and which hills? To solve this problem he will
often lay his map on the table, and while scanning it with
joyful anticipation he will study the various guide books

which describe this enchanting country. There he will *read* what their authors have so lucidly written, but much will inevitably be left to his imagination.

It is here that my long experience of the Lakeland Peaks will help him to solve these difficulties, for by consulting this volume (in conjunction with my other works devoted to this district) he will not only be able to choose his centre with certainty, his routes to the peaks in the vicinity in accordance with his powers as a climber, and his subjects for the camera if he happens to be a photographer, but he will also be able to *see* beforehand through the medium of my camera studies precisely the type of country that will satisfy every one of his personal tastes.

Equipment

If our embryo mountaineer is wise, he will give due consideration to the question of equipment, for he would be foolish to venture on to the hills in all sorts of weather without proper boots and clothing, to say nothing of the other useful incidentals which I shall enumerate later.

Boots are, of course, the most important item and in the course of 50 years climbing in Lakeland I have noticed in the last decade a great improvement in the footwear worn by walkers; for gone are the remnants of unserviceable shoes which at one time could be found in places like Aaron Slack and the bed of Rossett Gill, whereas nowadays proper climbing boots are almost universally worn. The good ones are expensive, but those who can afford the best will be more than repaid in the long run by their comfort and service. For instance, my last pair was made by Robert Lawrie over ten years ago and today they are in splendid condition after rough wear in Britain and the Alps. Most makers adhere to a pattern that has proved to be successful. The uppers are in one piece of pliable leather, stitched at the heel and fit the ankle like a glove. The boot has plenty of room in the toes which means that when descending steep slopes and scree the feet are not forced into the toecap. Moreover, they are usually padded round the ankles where most friction occurs. Most climbing boots have Vibram Soles which have both advantages and disadvantages; they are silent on the roads, easier on the feet on *dry* rock, but on ice, wet rock or mossy slabs they can be a handicap to rapid progress because the utmost care becomes imperative to avoid a slip, which in an exposed situation might result in a twisted or broken ankle.

In order to prepare for any eventuality it might be advisable to possess two pairs of climbing boots, one with Vibrams and the other with nails as illustrated herein. Strong nylon laces are vital and there is a wide choice which can be inspected in any mountaineering shop.

Makers of climbing footwear, are always trying to improve upon the normally used type, and the latest to come up with a boot and shoe that promises well is Karrimor. After innumerable experiments a design has been evolved, known as K-SB, that is light in weight, non-slip on either grass or rock. Even the elegant shoes are ideal for the fell walker and smart enough for casual wear. I have worn a pair of K-SB Trail and found them the most comfortable in my long experience.

Nailing is of paramount importance though nowadays on the decline, but there are so many varieties to satisfy so many diverse tastes that if they were all seen by the buyer at the time of purchase, much confusion and indecision might result. I thought it would simplify matters if I included a photograph of my own nailing, which experience has shown to be satisfactory for ordinary fell walking. Any well-known maker of climbing boots will, on request, nail them to this pattern, which is as follows:

Three No. 6 Tricouni round the toe of each boot.
Clinker in pairs round both edges of the sole.
Large muggers well distributed over both sole and waist.
No. 1 Tricouni near each edge of the waist.
Malleable serrated capping on the front edge of each heel.
Overlapping clinkers on the rim of the heel, and also spaced singly round the sides of the heel. One mugger in the centre of each heel.

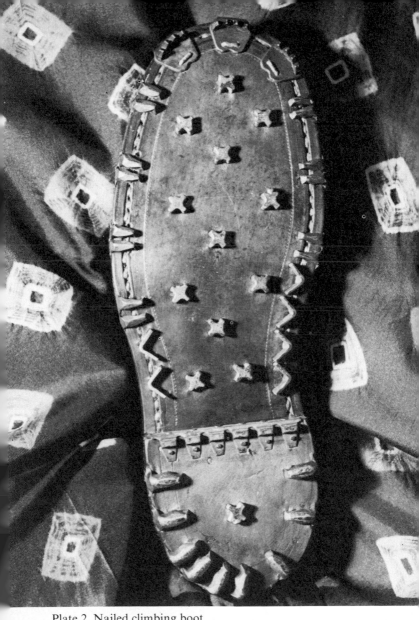

Plate 2 Nailed climbing boot

Stockings and socks are worthy of some attention and one of
each worn together ensure comfort and warmth and reduce
undue friction. The *colour* of these items may be important
and for the last two decades I have worn *red* ones because in
case of accident this colour can be seen at a great distance,
and in consequence would facilitate location and subsequent
rescue.

Clothes are perhaps a matter of personal taste, and there are
still a few rock climbers who delight in wearing their oldest
clothes or cast-off suits, sometimes with brilliant patches as a
decoration. But there is more protection when wearing a
properly made *Alpine Jacket* of which there are a variety of
patterns and colours, and one of the smartest for summer
wear on the hills is a Berghaus Alpen Lovat. They are usually
made from closely woven cotton of double texture at the main
points of friction. They are windproof and reasonably
waterproof and perfectly so if treated with silicone. The better
models have four pockets, of which two are large enough to
accommodate maps which are then kept dry. A skirt is now
made to most types, and in heavy rain keeps moisture from
percolating on to the small of the back. In the more expensive
models there is a small opening below the back of the neck to
accommodate a hood when not in use. Outside belts are no
longer worn because they might put a rock climber off balance
by inadvertently catching on a tiny excrescence of crag. They
are now universally replaced by a draw cord which runs in a
groove between the double-texture cloth. This type of Alpine
Jacket has a zip fastener down the front and goes well up into
the neck, whereas *Anoraks* are made in one piece, with a large
kangaroo pocket at breast height and a short zip only at the
neck, together with a throw-back hood with draw cord. Nylon
is now replacing cotton in some types. For climbers who
prefer a smart garment for use in cold weather on the tops, I
have found nothing better than a Pointfive High Sierra Jacket
with double open ended zips, which is very light and warm in
severe weather and not unlike the modern *Duvet*. In heavy

rain further protection is advisable and there is nothing better than a Gore-Tex Mistral which gives the best protection as it keeps out the rain and allows the perspiration to evaporate through the material. In view of the rapid changes of temperature which takes place in the hills, it is always advisable to wear a string vest and to carry spare *Pullovers*. Those made of light Shetland wool are much better than a heavy one, because the layers of warm air between them maintain the temperature, and the number worn can be easily adjusted in accordance with conditions. *Leg Gear* is a matter of choice, some swearing by trousers while others prefer plus twos. Personally I consider the latter more comfortable and, moreover, they allow more freedom about the feet. The *material* from which they are made is another consideration. Many climbers like corduroy, but I do not care for it, because it is made of cotton and therefore cold to the skin, and when it gets wet the material acts like a sponge and retains an excess of moisture. The weight about the legs then increases and is attended by much discomfort. On the other hand, hard-wearing and close-woven tweed is warm and light in weight and altogether more amenable for all hill conditions. *Puttees* are favoured by some mountaineers, more particularly for the support they are alleged to give to the muscles, but this contention is open to considerable doubt. In deep snow they certainly prevent it seeping into the boots, but if puttees are not worn this can also be prevented by wearing elastic waterproof anklets such as are often adopted by skiers. *Headgear* is another bone of contention. For years I wore none at all on the hills, and then after one summer day on the Napes I got a slight touch of sunstroke, the cool wind at the time disguising the power of the sun. I first wore a soft cloth hat that would not blow off in a high wind, but have now discarded it in favour of a bobcap which, in my view, is ideal for the climber. Peaked caps do not look right and are rather frowned upon by the climbing fraternity, but so far as I can see there is very little objection to them, excepting that in rain the water runs down the back of the neck. Balaclavas are indispensable in winter and there is no other headgear to equal them for comfort and warmth.

Gore-Tex. For the past few years Berghaus has been conducting research and development work on lined and vented anti-condensation garments. The Berghaus "Mistral" range is the end result and is, possibly, unique.

The advent of Gore-Tex 3 years ago opened up new possibilities in waterproofing clothing and was investigated eagerly. Briefly, Gore-Tex is a micro porous film which is laminated between the inner and outer layers of fabric. This film with 9 billion pores per square inch, discriminates between water as a vapour (individual molecules of water) and water as a liquid (hundreds of thousands of individual molecules bonded together in each drop). The tremendous number of pores allows water vapour to pass through freely because the pores are about 700 times larger than a water molecule, but "filters" out the liquid water, each drop being about 20,000 times larger than a Gore-Tex pore.

This means that internal body vapour is allowed to escape, keeping the wearer dry and comfortable, while being protected from wind and rain.

The original two layer laminate was effective as a waterproof, condensation free material, but became discoloured in areas of greatest pressure. The present Gore-Tex fabric has a third layer, a nylon scrim dyed to the same colour as the nylon taffeta. This tackles the problem of discolouration successfully, with the additional benefits of giving a more comfortable feel to the finished garment and making the fabric weldable.

In Britain, a hydrostatic head, or entry pressure, of 150 cms, i.e. 2.13 psi has been considered adequate for the fabric of mountain garments. The present Gore-Tex fabric now stands a hydrostatic head of over 60 psi, i.e. 4,225 cms, when new yet breathes as well as dry ventile garments even in wet conditions.

Abrasion tests have shown that there is no difference

between Gore-Tex nylon and p.u. or neoprene proofed nylon of the same weight. In addition, in terms of tear strength, the Gore-Tex nylon has between 2–4 times the strength of p.u. or neoprene proofed nylons. Each seam has been considered carefully and the best method of construction applicable to its position and function has been used.

Rucksacks are a necessary item of kit and may be obtained in a variety of shapes, sizes and weights. If all one's belongings are carried from place to place a large one is essential, otherwise a small light pattern should give satisfactory service. Some prefer those having a light metal frame which keeps the sack off the back and so allows plenty of ventilation.

A one-inch Map of the district should be the guide and friend of all who climb the Lakeland Peaks. There are two of outstanding merit: that issued by the Ordnance Survey has contours at intervals of fifty feet and the latest edition is admirably shaded to give a clear indication of the topography of the landscape; whereas Bartholomew's contours are at intervals of 250 feet and with an attractive layer system of colouring. Dissected maps mounted on linen are more easily handled out of doors but their present cost is so prohibitive that their general use is declining. However, a recent issue of four Leisure Maps by the Ordnance Survey on a scale of 1:25,000 cover almost the whole district and will replace the old 2½ inch series. They are expensive but the finest now available to both climber and fell walker.

A Compass should always be carried in the hills, despite the fact that it may not be needed in clear weather if the ground is familiar. In mist, however, all mountains become wrapped in deeper mystery with the disappearance of well-known landmarks, and if the climber is off the beaten track he may well find himself in difficulties without one. A good compass is not a cheap item of equipment, but it is money well spent.

Mountain photographers should note that certain types of

exposure meter containing a magnet may deflect the compass needle if the two are close together. Tests I have made indicate that at a distance of 9 inches N, 12 inches E and 18 inches S and W the magnetic north is deflected, and when the exposure meter is very near to the compass the needle spins round. Climbers should, therefore, test the two instruments and keep one well away from the other when in use, as in misty weather incorrect finding might result and so lead to unforeseen difficulties.

An Aneroid is a most useful instrument and perhaps a luxury to all save the explorer. A good one is a fairly reliable forecaster of the weather, and since it approximately indicates the altitude it may be a valuable aid in misty weather by helping to locate one's position with greater accuracy. The lower-priced instruments register up to a height of 10,000 feet. If you possess one, always make a point of adjusting the dial to the altitude of the starting-point of your climb, if it is known with certainty, and thereafter check it at any known station. Remember that when the barometer is falling the readings will be too high, and if rising they will be too low. In each case the error is about 100 feet for each 1/10 of an inch of rise or fall not due to change of altitude.

An Ice Axe is valuable and may be indispensable in snow climbing; moreover, it is a useful tool for glissading and its correct employment will ensure the safe and rapid descent of steep snow slopes. There are numerous makes, each of which has some slight variation in design of both pick and adze. A competent dealer will advise on the best type, which is largely governed by the length of shaft, weight and balance. A sling is a useful adjunct and may prevent the loss of the axe if it should slip out of the hand when in use.

In conclusion, I would advise everyone venturing on the hills at any time of year to carry the following items which could spell survival in extremely bad weather. 1. Map and Compass; 2. Torch and Whistle; 3. Spare Food and Clothing, including a large polythene bag; and 4. a small First Aid Kit.

Rock climbing

The Lakeland Peaks afford ample opportunities for the enjoyment of this exhilarating sport, but a novice should never attempt it without guidance and training. If you have a friend who is an experienced rock climber, ask him to tell you about its technique and the management of the rope, and at the first opportunity get him to lead you up some of the easy courses, when you will have the chance to put these theories into practice. If you have a steady head, good balance and can acquire the rhythm required for proficiency, he will soon notice it and lead you up routes of greater difficulty until finally you tackle the severes.

In the event of your becoming keen on rock climbing, you might wish to apply for membership of one of the climbing clubs of which the Fell and Rock is the acknowledged leader in the English Lake District. But owing to the great popularity of this sport this well known club, like many others in Britain, is so full that additional members are strictly limited at present. This club issues a series of comprehensive Climbing Guides which contain precise details of every known course of importance in the district.

The Lakeland centres

In the following list I have given the principal centres from which the Lakeland Peaks may be most conveniently climbed. But it should be borne in mind that strong walkers are often able to reach them from more distant centres, such as Youth Hostels, which are sometimes less conveniently situated. At the time of writing there were twenty-nine Hostels in the Lakeland region, but I have only cited those giving ready access to the major hill ranges.

Wasdale is the best centre in the district for rock climbing and is ideally situated for the courses on Scafell, Gable and Pillar. In view of its importance the accommodation available is much too limited, and apart from the Wastwater Hotel, now much improved, and Brackenclose, the latter belonging to the Fell and Rock Climbing Club, there are only four farmsteads. Burnthwaite stands in the shadow of the Great Gable at the foot of Sty Head; Wasdale Head Hall is just off the Burnmoor track at the head of Wastwater; and the Middle Fell and Rowhead are on the Black Sail side of the hotel. There is a Youth Hostel at Wasdale Hall, facing the Screes at the foot of Wastwater.

Ennerdale has very limited accommodation. The Angler's Inn at the western end of the lake was famous for its afternoon view of Pillar Fell, but alas, it has now been demolished; it was too far away from the hills to be a good centre and was thus mainly used by walkers touring the district. A bed may sometimes be found at one of the nearby farms. There are two Youth Hostels farther up the dale; the first is at Gillerthwaite Farm, one mile east of the head of the lake; and the second is Black Sail Hut, immediately under Haystacks. The latter is perfectly situated for the ascents of Pillar, Gable, Haystacks and High Stile.

Buttermere is a favourite Lakeland centre and very convenient for climbing High Stile, Dale Head and Grasmoor, but the Gable and Pillar are only within the range of strong walkers. This enchanting valley is resplendent with hotels and farms, from any of which the above ascents may be made as well as the circuit of either Buttermere or Crummock Water. Scale Hill and Loweswater are more distant, but make excellent centres for the ascent of Mellbreak and the Grasmoor group of hills. There are Youth Hostels at Buttermere and Honister Hause.

Newlands is well situated for the Grasmoor and Dale Head groups and numerous beds are available at the farms in the valley. The Youth Hostels at Keswick and Longthwaite give easy access to this neighbourhood.

Keswick brings many of the groups of hills within range by car, cycle or bus. It is perfectly situated for the ascent of Skiddaw and for the walk round Derwentwater, whilst Bassenthwaite, Blencathra, the Watendlath Fells and the Scawdell Fell—Catbells section of the Dale Head group are not too far away for the average pedestrian. There is a Youth Hostel in Station Road, Keswick.

Borrowdale is undoubtedly one of the best centres in all Lakeland, because it is not only well provided with hotels and every other type of accommodation, but is also admirably situated for the ascents of Dale Head, Haystacks, Great Gable, Glaramara, Great End, Scafell Pike and Bowfell, while even the Langdale Pikes are within range of a strong walker. Add to all these the accessibility of the Watendlath Fells and you have the cream of the Lakeland Peaks within reach of the energetic climber. There is a Youth Hostel at Longthwaite in a marvellous woodland setting near Rosthwaite and another at Barrow House near Grange.

Patterdale has plenty of accommodation throughout the

valley from Glenridding to Brothers Water and Low Hartsop
and comprises hotels, boarding houses and farms of all types.
In addition to the lovely scenes round Ullswater it is the best
base for the ascents of Helvellyn and Fairfield, and a good
one for High Street. Howtown is also well situated for the
latter range of hills, as well as for the lower reaches of the
lake. There is a Youth Hostel at Goldrill House, Patterdale,
and at Greenside, Glenridding, while the Fell and Rock Club
have a splendid hut near Brothers Water.

Mardale has now very little accommodation apart from the
excellent Haweswater Hotel, unless the farms towards
Bampton are patronised. It is admirably placed for the ascents
of High Street and Harter Fell, whilst the Shap Fells are also
within reach.

Long Sleddale, Kentmere and Troutbeck are extensive valleys
with a variety of accommodation, and the farmsteads at their
heads are in close proximity to the High Street and Ill Bell
ranges. Those situated in the last-named valley are convenient
for the ascent of Wansfell and for the walks round the upper
reaches of Windermere. There is a Youth Hostel at High
Cross Castle, Troutbeck, and others in Ambleside and
Kendal.

Ambleside and Grasmere are splendid centres for those using a
car, cycle or bus for transport to the more distant hills.
Without such conveniences the walker is restricted to the
Helvellyn range, Wansfell, Loughrigg, Silver How, the
Langdale Pikes, Helm Crag and the low hills about Easedale.
Both places have plenty of accommodation to suit all tastes
and are within reach of all the adjacent lakes and tarns. There
are Youth Hostels at Ambleside, two in Grasmere and
another at High Close, Loughrigg.

Langdale has ample accommodation from Skelwith Bridge
and Elterwater right up to the Old Hotel at the head of the

valley. Their situation is perfect for the ascents of the Langdale Pikes and Bowfell, while even the Coniston Fells, Scafell Pike and the Gable may be climbed by strong walkers. There is a Youth Hostel at Elterwater and members of the Fell and Rock Climbing Club have accommodation at Raw Head Farm. A welcome development is the transformation of Stickle Barn at the New Dungeon Ghyll Hotel, which now has a bar, self-service licensed grillroom and cafeteria specially designed to cater for the needs of walkers and climbers in any weather.

Coniston has numerous hotels and boarding houses, while farms are dotted about in the nearby valleys. These are well situated for access to the Coniston Fells, Tarn Hows and Hawkstead, to say nothing of the many adjacent lakes. There are Youth Hostels in Coniston (two) and at Esthwaite Lodge, Hawkshead.

Dunnerdale is rather too distant for access to the higher hills in the district, save the Coniston group and Harter Fell, Eskdale. There are hotels at Ulpha and Seathwaite, together with numerous farms as high up the dale as Cockley Beck. There is a Youth Hostel at Black Hall Farm, Seathwaite.

Eskdale is a splendid base for the Scafell and Bowfell ranges and affords one of the finest approaches to them both. Eskdale Green and Boot have a fair amount of accommodation, the Woolpack Inn being the highest hotel in the valley, and Taw House and Brotherikeld its two most remote farmsteads. Hard Knott and Harter Fell are easily reached from them all, but the two main groups involve a long day on the hills. There is a Youth Hostel high up the valley.

The Lakeland Peaks
141 Routes of ascent

The Scafell Group Map 1
SCAFELL PIKE
1. Wasdale, Brown Tongue and Mickledore
2. Wasdale, Brown Tongue and the Lingmell Col
3. Sty Head and Piers Ghyll
4. Sty Head and the Corridor
5. Esk Hause and Broad Crag
6. Brotherilkeld, Esk Falls and Rake Gill
7. Taw House, High Scarth Crag, Cam Spout and Mickledore

SCAFELL
8. Wasdale, Brown Tongue and Lords Rake
9. Sty Head, the Corridor and Hollowstones
10. Brotherilkeld, Esk Falls, Cam Spout and Mickledore
11. Taw House, High Scarth Crag and Cam Spout Crag
12. Woolpack Inn, Stony Tarn and Slight Side
13. Burnmoor direct

GREAT END
14. Sty Head and Skew Gill
15. Esk Hause direct

LINGMELL
16. From the Lingmell Col
17. From Brackenclose direct

The Gable Group Map 2
GREAT GABLE
18. Wasdale, Gavel Neese and the Sphinx Ridge
19. Wasdale, Gavel Neese and Beck Head
20. Ennerdale and Windy Gap
21. Honister and Green Gable

22 Seatoller and Gillercombe
23 Seathwaite, Sty Head and Aaron Slack
24 Sty Head and the Breast Track
25 Sty Head and the Climbers' Traverse

KIRKFELL
26 Wasdale and Beck Head
27 From Wasdale direct
28 Wasdale and Black Sail
29 Honister and Moses Trod

GLARAMARA
30 Rosthwaite and Thornythwaite Fell
30a Over Rosthwaite Fell
31 Langstrath and Esk Hause
32 Grain Gill and Esk Hause
33 Sty Head and Esk Hause

The Pillar Group Map 3

PILLAR
34 Wasdale and the High Level Route
35 Wasdale and Pillar Fell
36 Wasdale, Mosedale and Wind Gap
37 Wasdale, Dore Head and Red Pike
38 Overbeck and Red Pike
39 Netherbeck and Scoat Tarn
40 Ennerdale and Haycock
41 Gillerthwaite, Haycock and Scoat Fell
42 Ennerdale, Steeple and Wind Gap
43 Ennerdale and the Pillar Rock

YEWBARROW
44 Dore Head and Stirrup Crag
45 Overbeck and the Great Door

The High Stile Group Map 4

46 Buttermere and Scale Force

47 Buttermere and Ruddy Beck
48 Buttermere and Sour Milk Gill
49 Buttermere and Birkness Combe
50 Buttermere and Scarth Gap
51 Warnscale Bottom and Haystacks
52 Honister Hause and Haystacks
53 Gillerthwaite and Red Pike
54 Ennerdale and Starling Dodd

Dale Head Group Map 5
55 Rosthwaite and the Lobstone Band
56 Honister direct
57 Buttermere and Robinson
58 Newlands and Robinson
59 Newlands and Hindscarth
60 Newlands Beck and Dale Head Tarn
61 Keswick and Catbells
62 Grange and Castle Crag

The Grasmoor Group Map 6
63 Braithwaite and Grisedale Pike
64 Stair and Causey Pike
65 Buttermere and Wandope
66 Lanthwaite Green and Gaskell Gill
67 Whiteside and Hobcarton Pike

Skiddaw and Blencathra Map 7
SKIDDAW
68 Latrigg and Jenkin Hill
69 Millbeck and Carl Side

BLENCATHRA
70 Scales and Sharp Edge
71 Threlkeld and Hall's Fell Top
72 Keswick and the River Greta

Helvellyn Group Map 8

73 Patterdale and Swirral Edge
74 Patterdale and Striding Edge
75 Grisedale and Dollywaggon Pike
76 Grasmere and Grisedale Tarn
77 From Wythburn
78 Thirlspot and White Side
79 The Sticks Pass and Raise
80 Glenridding and Keppel Cove

Fairfield Group Map 9

81 Ambleside and Scandale Fell
82 Rydal and Nab Scar
83 Grasmere and Stone Arthur
84 Grasmere and Grisedale Tarn
85 Patterdale and St Sunday Crag
86 Patterdale and Deepdale
87 Patterdale and Dovedale
88 Brothers Water, Caiston Glen and the Scandale Pass
89 The Kirkstone Pass and Red Screes

The High Street Group Maps 10 and 11

HIGH STREET—NORTH Map 10

90 Patterdale and Pasture Beck
91 Patterdale and Hayes Water
92 Patterdale and Angle Tarn
93 Howtown and Weather Hill
94 Mardale and Measand Beck
95 Mardale and Kidsty Pike
96 Mardale and Rough Crag
97 Mardale and Nan Bield

HIGH STREET—SOUTH Map 11

 98 Kentmere and Nan Bield
 99 Troutbeck and Ill Bell
100 Troutbeck and Thornthwaite Crag

HARTER FELL–MARDALE
101 From Nan Bield
102 Mardale and Gate Scarth Pass
103 Long Sleddale and Gate Scarth

The Langdale Pikes Map 12
104 By Mill Gill
105 By Pavey Ark
106 By Dungeon Ghyll
107 Mickleden and the Stake Pass
108 Rosthwaite and the Stake Pass
109 Greenup and High White Stones
110 Dock Tarn and Ullscarf
111 Wythburn and Greenup
112 Grasmere and Far Easedale
113 By Easedale Tarn
114 By Silver How

The Bowfell Group Map 13
BOWFELL
115 Esk Hause and Esk Pike
116 Rossett Gill and Ewer Gap
117 By the Band direct
118 By the Band and Three Tarns
119 Brotherilkeld and Lingcove Beck

CRINKLE CRAGS
120 From Three Tarns
121 By Hell Gill
122 By Crinkle Gill
123 By Browney Gill
124 Wrynose and Cold Pike

PIKE O' BLISCO
125 Langdale and Kettle Gill
126 Little Langdale and Fell Foot
127 From Red Tarn

The Coniston Group Map 14

CONISTON OLD MAN
128 By the Quarries
129 By Goats Water
130 Walna Scar and Brown Pike
131 Seathwaite and Walna Scar
132 Seathwaite and Grey Friar
133 Wrynose, Carrs and Swirl How
134 Little Langdale and Wetherlam
135 Tilberthwaite Gill and Wetherlam
136 Coniston and Wetherlam

HARTER FELL–ESKDALE
137 Eskdale and Penny Hill
138 From Hard Knott Pass
139 From Birks Bridge
140 Seathwaite and Grassguards

Heights of the Peaks
In feet

1	3,210	Scafell Pike	25	2,698	Hart Crag
2	3,162	Scafell	26	2,687	Steeple
3	3,116	Helvellyn	27	2,649	Lingmell
4	3,054	Skiddaw	28	2,643	High Stile
5	2,984	Great End	29	2,634	High Raise
6	2,960	Bowfell			(High Street)
7	2,949	Great Cable	30	2,631	Coniston Old
8	2,928	Pillar			Man
9	2,917	Catchedicam	31	2,631	Kirkfell
10	2,903	Esk Pike	32	2,631	Shelter Crags
11	2,889	Raise	33	2,630	Swirl How
		(Helvellyn)	34	2,619	Haycock
12	2,863	Fairfield	35	2,611	Brim Fell
13	2,847	Blencathra	36	2,603	Green Gable
		(Saddleback)	37	2,593	Grisedale Pike
14	2,837	Low Man	38	2,585	Harter Fell
		(Skiddaw)			(Mardale)
15	2,816	Crinkle Crags	39	2,575	Carrs
		(Long Top)	40	2,572	Allen Crags
16	2,810	Dollywaggon	41	2,569	Thornthwaite
		Pike			Beacon
17	2,807	Great Dodd	42	2,560	Glaramara
18	2,791	Grasmoor	43	2,560	Kidsty Pike
19	2,760	Scoat Fell	44	2,555	Dow Crag
20	2,756	St. Sunday	45	2,541	Red Screes
		Crag	46	2,537	Grey Friar
21	2,756	Stybarrow	47	2,533	Wandope
		Dodd	48	2,525	Hobcarton Pike
22	2,753	Eel Crag	49	2,502	Caudale Moor
		(Grasmoor)	50	2,502	Wetherlam
23	2,719	High Street	51	2,501	Slight Side
24	2,707	Red Pike			(Scafell)
		(Wasdale)	52	2,500	High White
					Stones

53	2,500	Sail	85	2,159	Whiteless Pike
54	2,500	Dove Crag	86	2,155	Scandale Fell
55	2,496	Mardale Ill Bell	87	2,154	Place Fell
56	2,479	Red Pike	88	2,143	Scawdel Fell
		(Buttermere)	89	2,143	Harter Fell
57	2,476	Ill Bell			(Eskdale)
58	2,473	Dale Head	90	2,126	Fleetwith Pike
59	2,443	High Crag	91	2,120	Base Brown
60	2,417	Robinson	92	2,096	Snarker Pike
61	2,415	Seat Sandal	93	2,085	Starling Dodd
62	2,403	Harrison Stickle	94	2,070	Honister Crag
63	2,400	Carl Side	95	2,058	Yewbarrow
		(Skiddaw)	96	2,058	Looking Stead
64	2,385	Hindscarth	97	2,035	Walna Scar
65	2,380	Clough Head	98	2,019	Great Borne
66	2,370	Ullscarf	99	2,000	Causey Pike
67	2,359	Froswick	100	1,969	Black Combe
68	2,344	Brandreth	101	1,978	Illgill Head
69	2,333	Branstree	102	1,887	Maiden Moor
70	2,323	Pike o' Stickle	103	1,750	Haystacks
71	2,317	Whiteside	104	1,725	Buttermere
		(Grasmoor)			Moss
72	2,309	Yoke	105	1,703	Border End
73	2,306	Bowscale Fell	106	1,676	Mellbreak
74	2,304	Pike o' Blisco	107	1,597	Wansfell
75	2,288	Pavey Ark	108	1,596	Grike
76	2,287	Grey Knotts	109	1,481	Catbells
77	2,287	Great Calva	110	1,422	Rowling End
78	2,270	Seatallan	111	1,348	Scope End
79	2,259	Cold Pike	112	1,300	Silver How
80	2,239	Brown Pike	113	1,299	Helm Cragg
81	2,205	Scar Crags	114	1,203	Latrigg
82	2,188	Caw Fell	115	1,167	Kinn
83	2,174	Weather Hill	116	1,100	Loughrigg
84	2,174	Carrock Fell			

Heights of the Passes
In feet

1	2,490	Esk Hause	13	1,450	Garburn
2	2,420	Sticks	14	1,400	Scarth Gap
3	2,100	Nan Bield	15	1,300	Floutern Tarn
4	1,995	Greenup Edge	16	1,290	Hard Knott
5	1,990	Walna Scar	17	1,270	Wrynose
6	1,950	Gate Scarth	18	1,190	Honister
7	1,929	Grisedale	19	1,096	Buttermere Hause
8	1,800	Black Sail			
9	1,750	Scandale	20	1,043	Whinlatter
10	1,600	Sty Head	21	977	Burnmoor
11	1,576	The Stake	22	782	Dunmail Raise
12	1,476	Kirkstone	23	523	Red Bank

Heights above O.D. of the Lakes and Tarns
In feet

1	2,356	Red Tarn (Helvellyn)	26	1,383	Hayes Water
2	2,340	Three Tarns	27	1,350	Levers Water
3	1,960	Sprinkling Tarn	28	1,322	Dock Tarn
4	1,955	Greycrag Tarn	29	1,320	Greendale Tarn
5	1,949	Scoat Tam	30	1,300	Lingmoor Tarn
6	1,900	Scales Tarn	31	1,250	Floutern Tarn
7	1,842	Blind Tarn	32	1,230	Seathwaite Reservoir
8	1,800	Angle Tarn (Rossett)	33	1,200	Alcock Tarn
9	1,786	Low Water (Coniston)	34	1,017	Skeggles Water
			35	1,000	Stony Tarn
10	1,763	Grisedale Tarn	36	980	Greenburn Tarn
11	1,739	Red Tarn (Crinkles)	37	973	Kentmere Reservoir
12	1,700	Bleaberry Tarn	38	950	Gurnal Dubs (Potter Fell)
13	1,650	Dale Head Tarn	39	915	Easedale Tarn
14	1,650	Innominate (Haystacks)	40	850	Harrop Tarn
			41	847	Watendlath Tarn
15	1,646	Goats Water	42	832	Burnmoor
16	1,600	Angle Tarn (Patterdale)	43	790	Haweswater
			44	766	Devoke Water
17	1,600	Low Tarn (Wasdale)	45	724	Siney Tarn
			46	700	Blea Tarn (Boot)
18	1,600	Tarn at Leaves	47	700	Eel Tarn (Woolpack Inn)
19	1,588	Blea Water			
20	1,580	Black Beck Tarn	48	617	Tarn Hows
21	1,562	Blea Tarn (Watendlath)	49	612	Blea Tarn (Langdale)
22	1,540	Stickle Tarn	50	578	Thirlmere
23	1,528	Codale Tarn	51	536	Beacon Tarn
24	1,484	Small Water	52	520	Brothers Water
25	1,430	Sty Head Tarn	53	476	Ullswater

54	397	Lowes Water	61	223	Bassenthwaite
55	368	Ennerdale Water	62	217	Esthwaite
56	340	Little Langdale Tarn	63	204	Grasmere
			64	200	Wastwater
57	329	Buttermere	65	187	Elterwater
58	321	Crummock Water	66	181	Rydal Water
			67	143	Coniston Water
59	308	Loughrigg Tarn	68	138	Blelham Tarn
60	244	Derwentwater	69	130	Windermere

Mountain photography

I have already written and lectured extensively on this fascinating branch of photography, and in *Lakeland Through the Lens*, *Snowdon Holiday* and *Climbing with a Camera* I included notes on its application to the mountains of these two regions. But since all three volumes have been out of print for some years, it may be useful to give a summary of the essentials as almost every climber now carries a camera and is anxious to improve his snapshots. Moreover, I receive innumerable requests for tips from mountaineers who collect my works, and the following information may incidentally relieve me of much voluminous correspondence.

1 **The ideal camera for the mountaineer** is undoubtedly the modern miniature owing to its compact form, quick manipulation, great depth of focus, variety of lenses and thirty-six frames on each spool of film. While these instruments are represented in their best and most expensive type by the Leica, Pentax and Nikon series, it does not follow that other less costly makes will not give good photographs. Some year ago I had the opportunity of making a comparative set of colour transparencies with the Leica and a camera that then sold retail for about £12, and had I not been critical I should have been satisfied with the latter; for if you require a camera for your own pleasure and merely wish to show the prints or transparencies to your friends, then why pay over £100 for the instrument? In any case, I recommend that you consult your local dealer who will be happy to demonstrate the differences between the various makes and prices.

2 **The lens** is the most important feature, and the best of them naturally facilitate the perfect rendering of the subject. A wide aperture is not essential, because it is seldom necessary to work out of doors at anything greater than F/4.5. It is

advisable to use the objective at infinity in mountain photography because overall sharpness is then obtained, and to stop down where required to bring the foreground into focus. It is in this connection that the cheaper camera, which of course is fitted with an inexpensive lens, falls short of its more costly competitors; for the latter are corrected for every known fault and the resulting photographs are then not only more acceptable for enlarged reproduction but also yield exhibition prints of superlative quality.

Three lenses are desirable in this branch of photography: 1. a 28 mm or 35 mm wide angle; 2. a standard 50 mm which is usually supplied with most cameras; and 3. a 90 mm long focus. These cover every likely requirement: the wide angle is most useful when *on* a mountain or lofty ridge; the 50 mm encompasses the average scene, such as fell and dale; and the long focus is an advantage when the subject is very distant.

An analysis of their use in this region is as follows:

Wide angle	45 per cent
Standard	50 per cent
Long focus	5 per cent

3 **A lens hood** is an indispensable accessory, because it cuts out adventitous light and increases the brilliance and clarity of the picture. Many climbers have the illusion that this gadget is only required when the sun is shining and that it is used to keep the direct rays out of the lens when facing the light source. While its use is then imperative, they overlook the fact that light is reflected from many points of the hemisphere around the optical axis, and it is the interception of this incidental light that is important.

4 **A filter** is desirable, especially for the good rendering of skyscapes. A pale orange yields the most dramatic results, providing there are not vast areas of trees in the landscape in which all detail would be lost. It is safer to use a yellow filter, which does not suffer from this defect, and with autumn colours, a green filter is very effective. *The exposure factors* do

not differ materially, and in view of the wide latitude of modern black-and-white film the resulting slight differences in density can be corrected when printing. *For colour work* a skylight filter, formerly known as a Wratten 1A, is useful for reducing the intensity of the blues and for eliminating haze but nowadays colour film seldom requires its use.

5 **Panchromatic film** is to be preferred for landscapes, and the speed of modern types has been increased substantially, so much so that those having a Weston or ASA meter rating of up to 125 will yield grainless negatives providing they are processed with the developer that is recommended by the makers.

6 **Exposure and development** are co-related. From May to September with bright sunlight and well-distributed clouds, films of the above speed require an average exposure of 1/250th of a second at an aperture of F/8 or 11 with a 2 × yellow filter, processed with a fine-grain developer for 8 minutes at a temperature of 68°F. Such negatives should be brilliantly clear and not too contrasty, and they will print on normal paper.

7 **The best time of year** for your photography among the Lakeland Peaks is the month of May. A limpid atmosphere and fine cumulus are then a common occurrence and less time is wasted in waiting for suitable lighting. Colour work at this time is also satisfactory because the landscape still reveals the reds of the dead bracken, which, however, disappear in June with the rapid growth of the new fresh green fronds. Nevertheless, the most dramatic colour transparencies are obtained during the last week in October because the newly dead bracken is then a fiery red, the grass has turned to golden yellow, and the longer shadows increase the contrast between peak and valley.

8 **Lack of sharpness** is a problem that causes disappointment

to some amateurs, and they are often apt to blame the lens when the complaint is in fact due to camera shake. It is one thing to hold the instrument steady at ground level with a good stance and no strong wind to disturb the balance, while it is quite another problem in the boisterous breezes on the lofty ridges of Lakeland. When these conditions prevail, it is risky to use a lower speed than that indicated above, and maximum stability may be achieved by leaning against a slab of rock or in a terrific gale of wind by even lying down and jamming the elbows into the spaces between the crags; but foreground should never be sacrificed on this account. In calm weather a light tripod may be used, but in all other conditions, it is too risky to erect one and have it blown over a precipice!

9 **Lighting** is the key to fine mountain photography, and the sun at an angle of 45 degrees, over the left or right shoulder, will yield the required contrasts. These conditions usually appertain in the early morning or the late afternoon. If possible avoid exposures at midday with the sun overhead when the lighting is flat and uninteresting. Before starting on any climb, study the topography of your mountain so that full advantage can be taken of the lighting. Moreover, never be persuaded to discard your camera when setting out in bad weather, because the atmosphere in the hills is subject to the most sudden and unexpected changes, and sometimes wet mornings develop into fine afternoons, with magnificent clouds and limpid lighting. If your camera is then away back in your lodgings, you may live to regret the omission.

10 **The sky** is often the saving feature in mountain photographs since cloudless conditions or a sunless landscape seldom yield a pleasing picture and while fine sailing white cumulus are always a welcome crown to any mountain scene, they often last only a full morning which allows ample time to reach a selected viewpoint for a favourite subject. But really dramatic skies, with fast moving cloud shadows are rare and

Plate 3 The Scafell Pikes from Border End

can develop so rapidly that it is a matter of luck if you are near a superb viewpoint you know and from which you can capture the whole scene at its best. Such conditions prevailed in Upper Eskdale, dominated by the Scafell Pikes, as portrayed in Plate 3, which was taken from Border End above Hard Knott Pass, a belvedere that is perhaps the finest in all Lakeland. Readers of some of my earlier Art Volumes will have seen the same shot with cloudless skies and even in mist, but this one, exposed about 4 pm on a perfect afternoon in late October, is the finest in my collection. A coloured version in Kodachrome adorned the Jacket and Frontispiece of my *Climbing with a Camera*, published in 1963.

11 **Haze** is one of the bugbears in this branch of photography, and these conditions are especially prevalent among the Lakeland Peaks during July and August. If an opalescent effect is desired, this is the time of year to secure it, but while such camera studies may be favoured by the purist, they seldom appeal to the climber who prefers to see the detail he knows exists in his subjects.

12 **Colour photography** has been simplified in recent years by the introduction of cameras in which both exposure and aperture can be automatically adjusted to light conditions, and in consequence failures are rare. Owing to the narrow latitude of colour film correct exposure is essential if the resulting transparency is to approximate in hue to that of the landscape as seen by the eye. The only certain way to achieve success in all weather conditions is to *use a meter before making each exposure* and to be sure it is pointed at the same angle as the camera. This is most important, because if more sky is included in the meter than in the lens a shorter exposure will be indicated and this will result in an under-exposed transparency in which the colour will be unduly intensified, whereas if the two operations are reversed it will be weakened. Excellent results are obtainable with most makes of modern colour film, whose speed has been substantially increased in

recent years to ASA 25, 64 and 100. On the basis of ASA 25, an exposure of about 1/125 second at an aperture of F/8 in sunlight between 10 a.m. and 4 p.m. in the summer yields superlative transparencies. Whereas at high altitudes in snow 1/250 second at F8 is necessary. The correct exposures for other ASA speeds may be readily calculated from an exposure meter.

13 **Design or composition** is the most outstanding feature of a good camera study; that is, one that not only immediately appeals to the eye, but rather one that can be lived with afterwards. Everything I have so far written herein on this subject comes within the scope of *Technique*, and anyone who is prepared to give it adequate study and practice should be able to produce a good negative, and from it a satisfying print.

But to create a picture that far transcends even the best snapshot requires more than this and might well be described as a flair, or if you like a seeing eye that immediately appreciates the artistic merit of a particular mountain scene. And strangely enough those who possess this rare gift usually produce a certain type of picture which is indelibly stamped with their personality; so much so that it is often possible to name the photographer as soon as his work is displayed. And, moreover, while this especial artistic trait may be developed after long application of the basic principles of composition, the fact remains that it is not the camera that really matters, for it is merely a tool, but the person behind the viewfinder, who, when satisfied with the design of his subject, ultimately and quite happily releases the shutter.

To the painter, composition is relatively easy, because he can make it conform to the basic principles of art by moving a tree to one side of his picture, or by completely removing a house from the foreground, or by inducing a stream to flow in another direction, or by accentuating the real subject, if it happens to be a mountain, by moving it or by increasing or decreasing its angles to suit his tastes. A photographer on the other hand has to move himself and his camera here and there in order to get these objects in the right position in his viewfinder. When he moves to one side to improve the position of one of them, another is thrown out of place, or perhaps the lighting is altered. In many cases, therefore, a compromise is the only solution, because if he spends too much time in solving his problem the mood may change, when his opportunity would be lost. It is just this element in mountain photography that brings it into line with sport, and, like golf, it can be both interesting and exasperating. Of course, the critic can sit in a comfortable chair by a warm fire at home and pull a photograph to pieces. He does not, perhaps, realise that the person taking the picture may have been wandering about knee-deep in a slimy bog, or that a bitterly cold wind was sweeping across a lofty ridge and making his teeth chatter, or that the light was failing, or that he had crawled out on a rocky spur with a hundred-foot drop on either side to get his subject properly composed.

Assuming, therefore, both lighting and cloudscape are favourable, what are the essential features of good composition? In the first place, you must select a pleasing object that is accented by tonal contrast as the centre of interest; in the second, you must place this object in the most attractive position in the frame or picture space; and in the third, you must choose a strong and appropriate foreground. Or, in other words, when the weather is favourable the success or failure of your photograph will depend entirely upon the *viewpoint*.

Thus, if your subject happens to be Great Gable, I may be able to help you with a few hints about four of the illustrations in this book. It is generally agreed that the western aspect of this mountain is the finest and it looks its best on a sunny afternoon with high cloud overhead. But you must first decide whether you wish to take a picture of the majestic peak itself, or of its superb placing between the adjacent fells; the former depending upon the foregrounds available within close range, and the latter from a long distance.

Plate 4 Great Gable from Lingmell Beck

Let us begin with the nearest possible coign of vantage as shown in Plate 4, where Lingmell Beck provides the foreground interest and where a vertical frame and wide-angle lens are essential. But owing to the proximity of the mountain emphasis is concentrated on the Napes Ridges only, while the elevation and nobility of the peak is not revealed. If we go further back to near Burnthwaite we obtain by the same technique a rather foreshortened picture of it, where the only useful foreground consists of the wall and tree on the right. By retreating still further to Wasdale Green we get a more comprehensive view and can use a normal 50 mm lens, but as will be seen in Plate 5 the foreground lacks interest. If, on the other hand, we go still further back to the side-road leading to Brackenclose and Wasdale Head Hall, and walk beside the stream to a point near the confluence of Mosedale and Lingmell Becks, we shall discover a perfect foreground of trees and river together with a satisfactory view of our mountain at its correct elevation, as shown in Plate 6. An alternative viewpoint that reveals a similar elevation of the Gable, but with a different lead-in is portrayed in Plate 37, and those who are prepared to ascend Lingmell will secure the most dynamic shot, as shown in Plate 36. Finally, if you wish to photograph Great Gable from a distant coign of vantage there is no more effective foreground than Wastwater, where from the foot of the lake the eye is drawn straight to it and reveals its central situation between Yewbarrow and Lingmell, as shown in Plate 7. Whenever you take a shot at any of the Lakeland Peaks, remember that it will be improved not only by placing a lake, a stream, a bridge, a figure or a group of climbers in the foreground, but also on occasion by introducing a tree or cottage or some object whose size if known will impart both interest and scale to your picture.

In conclusion, I would call your attention to the dramatic possibilities of photographing sunsets in colour; for by placing a still or slightly rippling lake in the foreground you will immensely enhance the whole picture by capturing the colour reflected by water as well as that already appearing in the sky.

Plate 5 Great Gable from Wasdale Green

Plate 6 Great Gable from Lingmell Beck

Plate 7 Yewbarrow, Great Gable and Lingmell from Wastwater

Photography in the different groups

I have often been asked "What is the best view *of* such and such a mountain?" or "What is the most striking view *from* so and so?" These are difficult questions, because the answers depend so much on one's tastes, which are influenced in no small degree by atmospheric conditions on any particular occasion. The present volume seems to be a convenient medium for an attempt to offer some guidance on this very debatable question, and while there are doubtless many who will disagree with my opinions, I shall give them for what they are worth. Where possible I have appended references to appropriate examples already portrayed in one or other of my works, as follows:

LL : *Lakeland Through the Lens*
LH : *Lakeland Holiday*
LJ : *Lakeland Journey*
OLF : *Over Lakeland Fells*
CC : *Climbing with a Camera*
LP : *The Lakeland Peaks* (the present work).

The number indicates the plate in the particular volume, to which I have added the most suitable time of day for photographing the subject (G.M.T.). It should be noted that the examples given were not necessarily taken at the best time or season.

The suggestions are arranged according to the grouping system adopted throughout this work and under two headings: (1) The best pictorial views *of* the groups or their separate tops; (2) The most striking views *from* the groups. In both cases foreground interest is obviously of paramount importance since it bears a direct relationship to the pictorial rendering of the main subject.

The best pictorial views of the groups
The southern aspect of the Scafells
(*a*) From Border End. 11 a.m. or 4 p.m. LL 94; CC 68; LP 3.
(*b*) From Grey Friar to the north of the cairn. 11 a.m. or
    3 p.m. OLF 4; LP 232; CC62.
(c) From Harter Fell in Eskdale, on the western slopes to
    avoid Hard Knott. 11 a.m. or 3 p.m. LH 52; LP 23; CC 66.
(d) From Long Top on Crinkle Crags. 11 a.m. or 3 p.m.
    LJ 33; LP 216; CC 54.

Scafell Pike from Upper Eskdale. 11 a.m. or 3 p.m. LH 1;
CC 99.

Scafell from Lingmell. 7 p.m. onwards, May or June. LL 47 &
86; LP 13 & 29.

Great End from the western slopes of Glaramara. 9 a.m., May
or June.

Lingmell from The Corridor. 11 a.m., April, May or June.
LP 17 & 18.

Great Gable
(*a*) From Wasdale, 6 p.m., May or June. LL 76; LH 50;
    OLF 35; LP 37; CC 72.
(*b*) From Lingmell. 6 p.m., May or June. OLF 32; LP 36;
    CC 106.
(*c*) From Haystacks. 7 p.m., June. LH 38. LP 102

Pillar from Green Gable. 11 a.m., May or June. LL 60; LP 88.

Yewbarrow from Netherbeck. 4 p.m. onwards, May or June.
LL 65; LH 48; LP 89.

High Stile
(*a*) From Lanthwaite Hill, 6 p.m., May or June, OLF 61;
    LP 91.

(*b*) From Dale Head. 11 a.m., May or June.
(*c*) From Robinson. 11 a.m., May or June. OLF 79.
Dale Head from Loweswater Village, any time of day.

Skiddaw
(*a*) From Lodore. 6 p.m., Spring to Autumn.
(*b*) From Castle Head. 6 p.m., May or June. OLF 85; LP 132.

Blencathra
(*a*) From Clough Head. 10 a.m. or 4 p.m.
(*b*) From the east. 11 a.m. LP 137.
(*c*) From St. John's Vale. CC 22.

Helvellyn
(*a*) From Birkhouse Moor. 11 a.m. OLF 87; CC 17.
(*b*) From Striding Edge. 11 a.m. LL 16; OLF 88; LP 147; CC 18.
(*c*) From St. Sunday Crag. 11 a.m.

Fairfield from High Street. 11 a.m. LP 167.

High Street from Kidsty Pike. 11 a.m. LP 176.

High Street from Harter Fell. CC 16; noon LP 182.

Harter Fell in Mardale from Haweswater. 10 a.m. LL 12;
OLF 106; LP 177; CC 15.

The Langdale Pikes
(*a*) From Elterwater. 11 a.m. or sunset. LL 95; CC 47.
(*b*) From Chapel Stile. 3 p.m. onwards, Spring or Autumn.
LL 96; LP 186; CC 55.

Bowfell
(*a*) From Eskdale. 11 a.m. or 4 p.m. LL 89; LH 59; LP 207.
(*b*) From Long Top, Crinkle Crags. 11 a.m. or 4 p.m. LJ 36;
LL 113; LP 203; CC 58.

Crinkle Crags
(*a*) From Red Tarn. 11 a.m. LJ 27 & 28.
(*b*) From Langdale. 9 a.m. LJ 26; CC 53.
(*c*) Long Top Buttress. 3 p.m. LJ 30.

Coniston Old Man from Coniston Water. 11 a.m. CC 55; from Torver. LP 219.

Dow Crag from Goats Water. 11 a.m. LL 118; LP 225.

Wetherlam from Tarn Hows. 11 a.m. LJ 8; LP 239.

Harter Fell in Eskdale from above the Woolpack Inn. 4 p.m. LH 55; LP 247; CC 65.

Harter Fell in Eskdale from Dunnerdale. 11 a.m. CC 73; LP 250.

The most striking views from the groups
Scafell Pike. Great Gable and Sty Head. 11 a.m. or 4 p.m. LP 48.

Scafell
(*a*) Grasmoor Hills and the Gable. 4 p.m. LH 65; CC 105.
(*b*) Mosedale from Deep Ghyll. 4 p.m. LP 27; CC 104.
(*c*) Gable and the Pinnacle from Deep Ghyll. 4 p.m. LP 28.
(*d*) South from the summit cairn. 6 p.m. onwards. LH 70.

Great End
(*a*) Borrowdale and Skiddaw. 11 a.m. or 3 p.m. LL 41.
(*b*) The Gable and Sty Head from the northern slopes. 4 p.m. LJ 76; LP 47; CC 97.

Lingmell
(*a*) The Gable. 4 p.m. onwards. OLF 32; LP 36; CC 106.
(*b*) Sty Head. 4 p.m. onwards. OLF 31; LL 1 & 2.
(*c*) Mickledore and Hollowstones. 6 p.m. onwards, May or June. OLF 34; LP 10.

(*d*) Scafell. 7 p.m. onwards, May or June. LL 47 & 86; LP 29; CC 104.

Great Gable
(*a*) Wastwater from the Sphinx Rock. 11 a.m. LL 80; LP 53; CC 10.
(*b*) The Grasmoor Hills. 11 a.m. or 3 p.m. LP 54.

Kirkfell
(*a*) The Scafells. 6 p.m. CC 82; LP 57.
(*b*) The Gable. 3 p.m. CC 81; LP 58.

Glaramara
(*a*) Borrowdale. 11 a.m. or 3 p.m. CC 30.
(*b*) The Gable. 11 a.m. LJ 72; CC 30; LP 68.
(*c*) The Langdale Pikes. 5 p.m. LJ 73.

Pillar
(*a*) West face of the Pillar Rock. 4 p.m. onwards. LL 71; LP 78; CC 80.
(*b*) East face of the Pillar Rock. 11 a.m. LL 70; LP 74; CC 78.
(*c*) The Central Fells from just below the Great Doup. 5 p.m. onwards.

Yewbarrow. The Scafells from the Great Door. 6 p.m. onwards. LL 75; LP 90.

High Stile. The Central Fells. 6 p.m. OLF 52; LP 99; CC 40.

Fleetwith Pike. The Buttermere Valley. 11 a.m. CC 37.

Dale Head
(*a*) Newlands and Skiddaw. 4 p.m. onwards. OLF 78; CC 43.
(*b*) Honister, High Stile and Buttermere. 11 a.m. LP 109; CC 44.

Grasmoor. The Central Fells. 6 p.m. onwards. OLF 65; LP 131; CC 46.

Skiddaw
(a) Derwentwater from Latrigg. 10 a.m. LJ 49 & 50.
(b) Derwentwater from Carl Side. 10 a.m.
(c) The Grasmoor Hills. 11 a.m. LJ 46.

Blencathra. Looking across the lateral spurs to Derwentwater. 11 a.m. LL 21; LP 141; CC 21, and CC 24 at 4 p.m.

Helvellyn
(a) Striding Edge from the Abyss. 11 a.m. OLF 91; LL 17; LP 148; CC 19.
(b) The western Panorama. Up to midday. OLF 90; LP 152.

Fairfield
(a) Ullswater from St. Sunday Crag. 6 p.m. OLF 101; LP 158; CC 20.
(b) Windermere from Nab Scar. 11 a.m. or 4 p.m.

High Street
(a) The western Panorama. 11 a.m. LP 167&168.
(b) Windermere from Thornthwaite Beacon. 11 a.m. or 4 p.m. LL 13.

Harter Fell in Mardale. Haweswater. 11 a.m. or 4 p.m. CC 16; LP 181

The Langdale Pikes
(a) Harrison Stickle from Pike o' Stickle. 3 p.m. LL 106; LP 194; CC 52.
(b) Gimmer Crag from Pike o' Stickle. 4 p.m. LL 107 & 108; LP 193; CC 51.
(c) Pavey Ark from Stickle Tarn up to 2 p.m. CC 52; LP 189

Bowfell. The Scafells. 11 a.m.

Crinkle Crags
(a) The Scafells. 11 a.m. LJ 33; LP 22 & 30; CC 54.

(*b*) Pike o' Blisco from Mickle Door up to noon. LJ 32; CC 57.

Pike o' Blisco. Great Langdale. 11 a.m. LJ 25.

Coniston Old Man. North-west to the Central Fells. 3 p.m. LP 222.

Grey Friar. The Scafells. 2. p.m. OLF 4; LP 232, CC 62.

Wetherlam. The Langdale Pikes from below Birk Fell. 11 a.m. or 3 p.m. LJ 20; LP 238.

Harter Fell in Eskdale. The Scafells and Upper Eskdale. 11 A.M. OR 3 P.M. LH 52; LP 23; CC 66.

Border End in Eskdale. The Lakeland Giants. 4 p.m. LL 94; CC 68; CC frontispiece in colour; LP 3.

Notes on the Routes

The Lakeland Peaks are divided into *fourteen Mountain Groups* for the sake of convenience and easy reference. They commence with the Scafells, because Scafell Pike is the highest mountain in England and its ascent the most popular. The groups then follow each other in clockwise sequence throughout the district and end with the Coniston Group and Harter Fell in Eskdale. *The Routes* to the reigning peak in each group are also arranged clockwise so that they fit into the general scheme and thus avoid undue cross reference. *Descents* have been purposely omitted because when the ascents are reversed they obviously answer this requirement. These arrangements facilitate the choice of those routes which connect up with one another to form a *Traverse* of two, or even three, groups in one expedition, but their length will naturally depend upon the powers of the climber. *The Panorama* from the reigning peak in each group is always described at the end of its first ascent. Many of the routes involve the traverse of subsidiary tops and the conspicuous features revealed from them are noted in passing, in spite of the fact that there may be a similarity in the views if the peaks are adjacent.

Distances and times

These problems always involve a certain amount of speculation in mountaineering and I have purposely omitted any detailed reference to them in this work. *The Distances* may be calculated approximately from the maps which are approximately one inch to the mile, but it should be borne in mind that a map mile may in fact be considerably more than that owing to the undulating nature of the ground. *The Times* depend not only upon the pace of each climber, but also upon the topography of the mountain as well as weather conditions. The best way to calculate them is to use the formula of Naismith, which allows one hour for every three map miles, plus half an hour for every 1,000 feet of climbing. This is fairly accurate for ordinary fell walking under good conditions, and while it includes reasonable halts for food and for viewing the mountain scene, it does not allow for bad weather, snow, rock climbing or photography, since the latter often involves much delay in finding the most effective foreground for any particular picture.

To make the application of this system clear, I will illustrate it by calculating the distance and time required for the circuit of the Helvellyn Horseshoe, which is described and portrayed in my *Over Lakeland Fells*.

It is four map miles from Patterdale to the summit of Helvellyn by way of Striding Edge (Route 74); two and a quarter miles of descent from the cairn to Grisedale Tarn (part of Route 75); three-quarters of a mile from here to the top of Fairfield (part of Route 84); and four miles back to Patterdale taking in Cofa Pike, Deepdale Hause and St. Sunday Crag (Route 85). This makes a total of eleven map miles, which according to the above formula will take approximately three and three-quarter hours.

Patterdale stands on the 500-feet contour, so this must be subtracted from the height of Hevellyn, $3,118 - 500 = 2,618$

feet, but since there is a drop of about 100 feet between the eastern top of Striding Edge and the Saddle, this must be added, which makes the ascent of the mountain 2,718 feet. The climb up to Fairfield from Grisedale Tarns adds another 1,100 feet, which makes the total now 3,818 feet, but there is a further ascent of 682 feet from Deepdale Hause to St. Sunday Crag, so that the total height to be scaled is 4,500 feet, which according to the above formula adds two and a quarter hours; thus allowing altogether six hours for the walk in good weather.

In this particular example the traverse of both Striding Edge and Cofa Pike would add something to the time, and as there is much of interest to see from all the tops a further allowance should be made for viewing these scenes. It would therefore be safe to say that if the climber left Patterdale at 10 a.m. he would be back in time for a bath before dinner.

Route finding in mist

In these not uncommon conditions it is imperative to know
with certainty your exact location on the map when mist
comes down to engulf you in gloom and to immediately note
the direction to be taken. If you are on a well cairned track no
difficulties should be encountered, but when this is not the
case you must estimate the distance to the next known point
and set a course accurately by using your companion as a
sighting mark. Keep him in view ahead while frequently
referring to the compass and use your aneroid to check the
rise and fall in the ground. If you are familiar with the
gradient this will help to control your direction, but take
nothing for granted; always trust the compass excepting when
among magnetic rocks, basaltic and gabbro formations such
as exist in the Coolins of Skye, and pay no attention
whatsoever to gratuitous advice as to the direction from
compassless companions. Avoid contouring a slope; if you do
this, you will no longer be master of your direction. It is
always advisable to go straight down and never diverge from
a supposed obstacle, because mist exaggerates both size and
distance.

Should you be in the unhappy position of having no
compass but *are familiar with the terrain* work your way down
slowly over grass but never enter a ravine or gully or
endeavour to descend a series of steep crags, whereas if you
are on a ridge keep to its declining crest and if it forks make
sure you take the known branch. If, on the other hand you are
alone on an uncairned track and also unfamiliar with the
ground, stay put until the mist clears sufficiently for you to
find your way. In these conditions you are in a very dangerous
situation because mist sometimes persists for days in
mountainous country. It is much better to practise map and
compass reading in clear weather so that in mist you will have a
reasonable chance of finding your way to safety.

Accident procedure

Distress signal. *Six* long flashes or *six* long blasts of a whistle in quick succession followed by a pause of one minute. This is repeated again and again until assistance is forthcoming.

The reply to this signal is in a similar vein; that is *three* flashes or blasts of a whistle followed by a pause of one minute, repeated again and again.

Brocken Spectres

These phenomena are confined to hill country, and in consequence may, with luck, be observed by any climber on the Lakeland Peaks, especially if he is on a ridge enclosing a combe filled with mist. They appear to be gigantic shadows seen on the mist and were first viewed on the Brocken in Germany, hence the name. but are said to be an optical illusion because the shadow is quite close and of actual size. It is usually only possible for each climber to see his own spectre.

Glories

These appear as a coloured ring round the shadow cast by the climber on the mist in similar circumstances. Each member of a climbing party can only see his own glory.

The Scafell group

Scafell Pike	3,210 feet	978 metres
Scafell	3,162 feet	964 metres
Great End	2,984 feet	910 metres
Lingmell	2,649 feet	807 metres
Slight Side	2,501 feet	762 metres
Esk Hause	2,490 feet	759 metres
Sty Head	1,600 feet	488 metres

The approach to Wasdale

The importance of Wasdale as a Lakeland climbing centre has been well known throughout the years and is due to the proximity of Scafell, Scafell Pike, Great Gable and Pillar. All these groups of hills display some of the finest subjects for both artist and photographer, and in my early days we all had to accept the lack of amenities at the hotel, just to be there on the spot. But today I am glad to say that the improvement in accommodation and food is immense and on a recent visit I was not only delighted with them but also with the excellence of the service.

However, to reach the hotel most climbers come by car and when the foot of the lake is revealed ahead they must be greatly impressed by the magnificence of the Screes, a strange feature that is unique in our British Hills. I felt therefore that the inclusion of just one photograph of them in this edition would be welcomed by readers, although the gully climbs and the charming walk over Illgill Head are omitted from this work.

Plate 8 The Wastwater Screes

Map 1
Scafell Group
Routes 1 to 17

Scafell Pike

Route 1. Wasdale, Brown Tongue and Mickledore. Leave
Wasdale by the Gosforth road, and after passing the old
school turn L through a gate where a finger-post points the
way across the fields. Cross the bridge over Lingmell Beck
and turn R, crossing the wall by some iron steps. The path
rises gently round the flanks of Lingmell with increasingly
extensive vistas along Wastwater to the Screes. When
Lingmell Gill comes into view ahead, bear L above it, and
after crossing the wall by some more iron steps advance above
the stream to the cairn at the foot of Brown Tongue. A well-
marked path ascends this steep spur with Pike's Crag looming
on the horizon. When the gradient eases off, Hollowstones
will be perceived ahead stretching across the great basin below
Pike's Crag. Bear R here and keep well below the precipices of
Scafell. Do not ascend the scree shoot on R, but go straight
ahead to Mickledore. The ascent of this ridge is the crux of
the climb and the easiest way to tackle it is by keeping to the
centre spur of grass as far as some projecting rocks. Skirt
these to the narrow neck of scree on R and cross it to join the
track below the Scafell precipices. This leads to the narrow
crest of Mickledore, where a path runs L and ascends the
maze of boulders strewn about Scafell Pike. The path divides,
that on L passing above Pike's Crag to descend to the
Lingmell Col, while the main one on R leads to the great cairn
on the Pike itself.

The panorama is extensive with uninterrupted views in all
directions. On a clear day all the engirdling hills can be seen
and the distant prospect comprises Skiddaw and Blencathra
to the north; the great Helvellyn range on the eastern horizon
and the Coniston Fells and Harter Fell to the south. Among
the more prominent of the nearer hills Pillar dominates the
north-western view, Gable rises across the confines of Sty
Head to the north with a glimpse of Derwentwater above the
Tarn. Bowfell appears, less interesting, to the south-east and
Scafell to the south-west. The western vista is striking with the

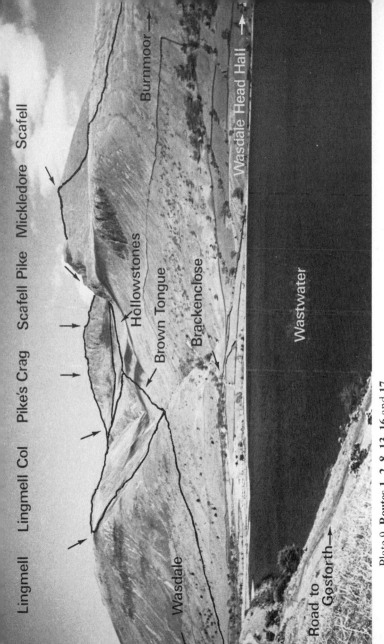

Lingmell   Lingmell Col   Pike's Crag   Scafell Pike   Mickledore   Scafell

Burnmoor

Hollowstones

Brown Tongue

Brackenclose

Wasdale Head Hall

Wastwater

Wasdale

Road to Gosforth →

Plate 9 **Routes 1, 2, 8, 13, 16** and **17**

Plate 10 **Routes 1** and **2** to the main Scafell Crags

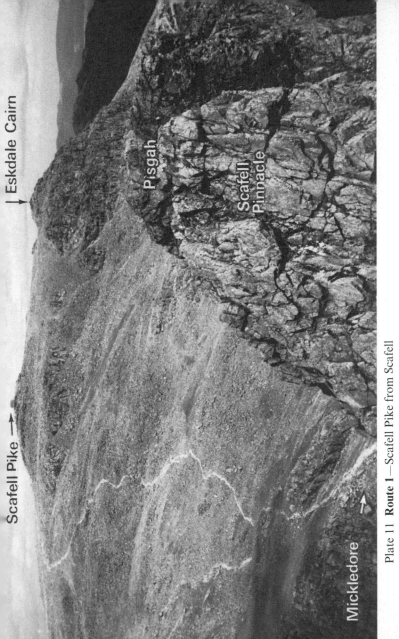

Eskdale Cairn

Scafell Pike →

Pisgah

Scafell Pinnacle

Mickledore

Plate 11 **Route 1**—Scafell Pike from Scafell

Plate 12 Route 1 — Climbers resting by the cairn on Scafell Pike

sea glittering away into the dim distance where the Isle of Man may be perceived in clear weather. The Eskdale Cairn is worth visiting because it reveals an amazing bird's-eye view of Upper Eskdale with the river 2,000 feet below.

Route 2. Wasdale, Brown Tongue and the Lingmell Col. This is a less arduous ascent than Route 1, but it follows the same course as far as the top of Brown Tongue. Bear to L here and follow a line of cairns which rise gently to the Lingmell Col on the north of Pike's Crag. On reaching it, a cairned track ascends the rough slopes on R which winds about over the easiest gradients and joins Route 1 again just below the cairn on the reigning peak.

Route 3. Sty Head and Piers Gill. Leave the large cairn by a track on the L of the Wasdale path, which takes a direct line for Skew Gill. On reaching the mouth of this conspicuous ravine, take the lower of the two tracks on the R which soon unfolds a prospect of Piers Gill straight ahead below Lingmell. Keep to the L of it and follow its precipitous retaining walls. The track is indistinct, so that the narrowest parts of its subsidiary rifts must be found to cross them in safety. This involves a slight divergence to the L from Piers Gill, but return to it where it bends sharply to the L and follow the edge of this section to its source. Here the well marked Guides Route comes in from the Corridor on the L, and after crossing the stream bear to the R for the dip on the horizon. This is the Lingmell Col, and now follow Route 2 on the L to the summit of Scafell Pike.

Note—Climbers coming from Wasdale need not ascend the well trodden stony path to Sty Head. They should leave it at the point where it begins to ascend, and instead pick up the rather indistinct track on the R which meanders over grass and boulders beside the beck. About a mile ahead cross the stream to a cairn and ascend the grassy zig-zags until Skew Gill appears ahead. Now make for this ravine and pick up the track on the R for Piers Gill, or for the Corridor as desired.

Pulpit Rock

Scafell Pike

Lingmell

Plate 13 The final section of **Route 2**

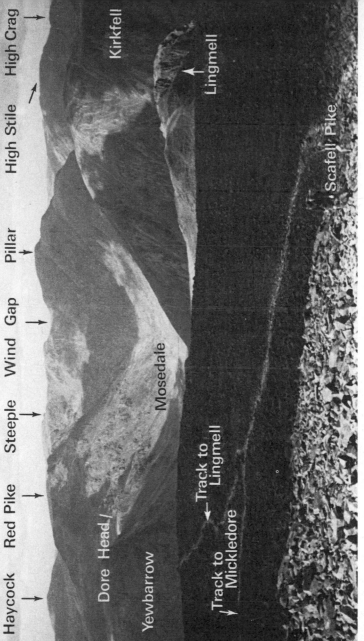

Plate 14 **Route 2** — The north-western prospect from the summit

Haycock   Red Pike   Steeple   Wind Gap   Pillar   High Stile   High Crag

Kirkfell

Lingmell

Scafell Pike

Dore Head

Mosedale

Yewbarrow

Track to Lingmell

Track to Mickledore

Plate 15 Sty Head—morning mists clearing from the Scafell Pikes

Great End →

Corridor Route ↗

Skew Gill

To Piers Gill

Sty Head

Wasdale Track

Plate 16 **Routes 3, 4** and **14** are well seen from just below Sty Head

Route 4. Sty Head and the Corridor. Follow Route 3 to Skew Gill, but take the steeper path out of it to L. The track rises sharply at first until the more level stretches of the Corridor are attained. Follow it to the junction above Piers Gill and then keep to Route 3 to the summit of Scafell Pike. Those wishing to take a short cut from the top of the Gill will scramble up the defile between Broad Crag and Scafell Pike and then join Route 5 to the summit of the latter. The views to the north from the Corridor are especially fine of Great Gable, where the maze of tracks leading to its summit may be easily perceived. There are also bird's eye views into Piers Gill on the R, together with a magnificent frontal view of the crags of Lingmell.

Route 5. Esk Hause and Broad Crag. This is one of the most clearly marked and well-cairned tracks in Lakeland. It leaves the shelter slightly south of west and rises gently to the dip on the horizon between Ill Crag on L and Long Pike on R. Just short of this little col there is a spring, the last place where a drink may be obtained on this route. The track goes up and down over a perfect maze of rough boulders with the Cairn on Scafell Pike rising above Broad Crag. After traversing this extensive plateau there is a sharp drop to the top of Rake Gill and then the path sweeps round to the large cairn perched on the roof of England.

Plate 17 **Route 4** crosses Piers Gill, at its exit on the R, immediately below the summit crags of Lingmell

Plate 18 **Route 3**—Lingmell and Piers Gill

Plate 19 Retrospect from **Route 5** near Esk Hause

Route 6. Brotherilkeld, Esk Falls and Rake Gill. Walk to the L of the farmyard of Brotherilkeld, situated near the foot of Hardknott Pass, and pick up the track well above the River Esk on L. Yew Crags tower above on R, and after passing below them drop down gradually to join the left bank of the stream. This sweeps round to L as far as the new packhorse bridge over Lingcove Beck. Cross it and ascend the grassy banks on R of Esk Falls, which cannot be seen to advantage from this side. Pass through Esk Gorge at the top of the Falls and turn sharp L at the bend in the river. Follow this with Scafell rising ahead and then at the small cataract which reveals Scafell Pike to the north keep to the right bank of the stream until about opposite Cam Spout. Now make for Esk Buttress and cross the river at any convenient spot. Pass below the precipices of this fine escarpment and then Rake Gill will be disclosed beyond it. Climb up beside the beck until the col is attained and then turn to the left and follow Route 5 to the summit. The views of the Upper Esk Basin unfolded after passing the above-mentioned cataract are some of the most profound in Lakeland. The great ridge is crowned by the giants of the district and forms a stupendous horseshoe from Slight Side in the west to Long Top in the east and includes Scafell, Scafell Pike, Ill Crag, Esk Pike and Bowfell.

Plate 20 **Route 6**—Esk Falls are revealed between two routes to Scafell Pike

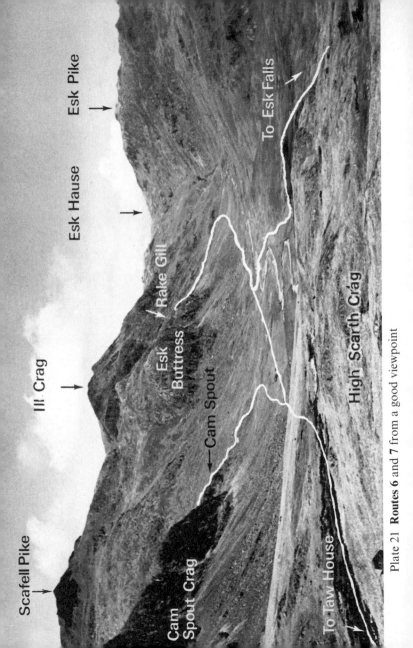

Plate 21 **Routes 6** and **7** from a good viewpoint

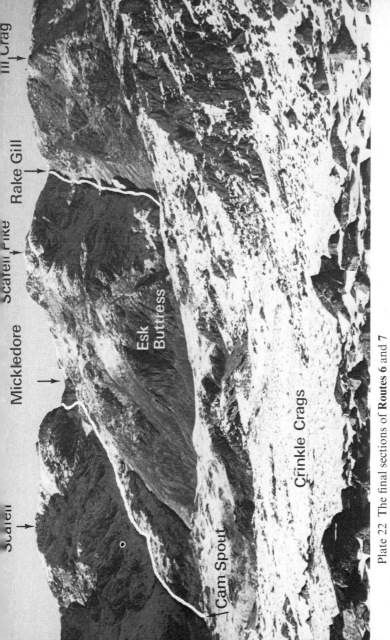

Plate 22 The final sections of **Routes 6** and **7**

Labels on image: Ill Crag · Rake Gill · Scafell Pike · Mickledore · Scafell · Esk Buttress · Cam Spout · Crinkle Crags

Route 7. Taw House, High Scarth Crag, Cam Spout and Mickledore. The farmstead may be reached from the main road in Eskdale by a rough cart track, but since the construction of a new footbridge over the River Esk at Brotherilkeld it is perhaps easier to park your car in the space on the L at the foot of Hard Knott Pass and walk the short distance to it. Now go through the gate at the back of the farm and follow the wall on the R to the old stone bridge over Cow Cove Beck. Thence bear L and ascend the steep grassy zig-zags which, on attaining the open fell, reveals Slight Side with High Scarth Crag immediately on its R. Hereabouts the path becomes very indistinct, but take a direct line for the small dip to L of High Scarth Crag. On attaining the little col the whole of Upper Eskdale is disclosed ahead. Down below on the left a sheepfold will be seen, and descend to this where the track from the river comes up on R. Follow the path below the shattered cliffs of Cam Spout Crag and at their northern terminus swing round to L, cross the stream emerging from Cam Spout and climb up on R of this rocky gorge. The path keeps close to the stream at the top and Mickledore will soon be seen on the horizon. Make for it, climb the loose scree and join Route 1 on the crest of the ridge.

Plate 23 **Routes 7, 10, 11** and **12** seen from Harter Fell

Long Top

Three Tarns

Bowfell

Esk Pike

Esk Hause

Scafell Pike

Slight Side

Scafell

Ill Crag

High Scarth Crag

Lingcove Beck

Esk Falls

Brotherilkeld

Taw House

To Stony Tarn

Harter Fell

Scafell

Route 8. Wasdale, Brown Tongue and Lords Rake. Follow Route 1 into Hollow Stones and then ascend the scree shoot on R which leads to the foot of Lords Rake. This is the narrow ravine on R at the top of the scree and it provides a good scramble to the skyline. Here take the track on the left which rises sensationally above the lower reaches of Deep Ghyll and is known as the West Wall Traverse. This leads into the gloomy recesses of Deep Ghyll itself where Scafell Pinnacle rises on L and Deep Ghyll Buttress on R. The rift is characterised by loose scree and great care is necessary in ascending it. The best course is usually on L where the rock is firmer and it leads to the skyline where the cairn on Scafell is seen ahead. Follow the rim of the chasm to L and scramble on to Pisgah, which unfolds one of Lakeland's most impressive mountain landscapes. It is worth while descending to the east as far as Broad Stand, but its negotiation should only be attempted by experienced rock climbers. Return to Pisgah and then walk over to Deep Ghyll Buttress, but do not attempt to descend to the north of this eminence. Walk up to the summit cairn for the view to the south, which comprises all the southern hills, in which Harter Fell is prominent, the sands of the Duddon beyond, and Morecambe Bay in the far distance.

Note—Climbers who wish to avoid the trying ascent of Deep Ghyll should continue to the end of Lords Rake and then turn L to scramble up the rough crags to the summit of Scafell.

Note—Erosion has made the ascent of Lords Rake dangerous for fell walkers, and until the loose boulders have been cleared it should be avoided.

— Scafell

Deep Ghyll

West Wall Traverse

Lords Rake

To Wasdale

Mickledore

Rakes Progress

Hollowstones

Plate 24 **Route 8** can only be photographed late on a summer evening

West Wall Traverse

Lords Rake

Broad Stand

Mickledore

Plate 25   The hardest and final section of **Route 8** to Scafell

Plate 26 The exit of **Route 8**

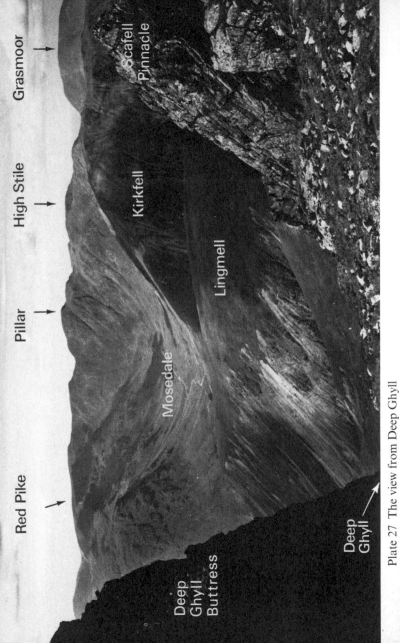

Plate 27 The view from Deep Ghyll

Plate 28 Looking back on the exit of Deep Ghyll

Blencathra

Skiddaw

Great Gable

Pisgah

Scafell Pinnacle

Lingmell

Deep Ghyll Buttress

Deep Ghyll

Route 9. Sty Head, the Corridor and Hollowstones. Follow
Route 4 to the Lingmell Col, keep below the precipices of
Pike's Crag on L and then pick up the rather indistinct track
above Hollowstones. Scafell rises ahead, and this route reveals
one of the best prospects of its savage precipices. Join Route 8
at the foot of the scree shoot leading to Lords Rake.

Route 10. Brotherilkeld, Esk Falls, Cam Spout and Mickledore.
Follow Route 6 as far as the cataract. Cross it and make for
the sheepfold. Pick up Route 7 as far as Mickledore and then
follow the track below the Scafell bastions into Lords Rake.
Keep to Route 8 for the summit.

Plate 29 **Route 9**

Route 11. Taw House, High Scarth Crag and Cam Spout Crag.
Follow Route 7 as far as the top of Cam Spout. Cross the
stream here and make for the edge of Cam Spout Crag,
crossing the boulder-strewn slopes to the south. There is no
track, but keep near the edge of the precipices, which unfold
impressive views of Upper Eskdale far below. As the ridge
narrows, bear to R slightly and then follow its crest until the
summit ridge is attained. Turn to R and keep to the broad
high ground which eventually leads to the cairn on Scafell.

Route 12. Woolpack Inn, Stony Tarn and Slight Side. Leave
the inn by the gate at the back and climb up the path until it
emerges on the shore of Eel Tarn, which, in June, is
beautifully decorated with water lilies. Pass round the far side
of this sheet of water and then bear to R, climbing gently in a
north-easterly direction until Stony Tarn appears below on R.
Forge ahead towards Slight Side, keeping well above Cow
Cove Beck on R. Ascend Slight Side and follow the broad
ridge which leads to the cairn on Scafell. A pleasant variation
starts opposite Wha House. Cross the stile and ascend the
winding path through the bracken. Pass through a sheepfold
and then follow the track beside a wall, known as the Terrace,
which eventually bears L to join the main path from the
Woolpack Inn. The lower reaches of this variation unfold
some fine views of Hardknott and Bowfell.

Route 13. Burnmoor direct. A well-marked track runs from
Wasdale to the Woolpack Inn, Eskdale, and also to Boot.
Leave it at any of the cairns on the Wasdale side well above
Burnmoor Tarn and make your own route to the summit of
Scafell which rises ahead to the east.

Plate 30 **Routes 10, 11** and **12** are well seen from Crinkle Crags

Great End

Route 14. Sty Head and Skew Gill. Follow Route 3 into Skew Gill and walk up the lower reaches of this impressive ravine. It bends round to L near the top and the exit provides a pleasant scramble. The easiest way out is on the extreme left and then steep rocks lead to the cairns on the summit of Great End. Before crossing the vast summit plateau, note the superb retrospect of Great Gable and Sky Head Tarn, with Grasmoor R of the peak. Consult Plate 16.

Route 15. Esk Hause direct. Leave the shelter by Route 5 and bear to R from the track after about 100 yards. The ascent is over rough boulders and the best views are obtained by keeping to the edge of the precipices. The cairns stand back on the left but they do not reveal the finest prospects. The panorama to the north is one of the most magnificent in Lakeland and is observed to the best advantage from the south exit of the Central Gully which splits the vast precipices on the northern aspect of the mountain where they drop away sensationally in the foreground. The dark waters of Sprinkling Tarn appear 1,000 feet below and the eye follows the dim recesses of Grain Gill and, after passing over the green strath of Borrowdale, skims the surface of Derwentwater to rest finally upon the noble form of Skiddaw on the distant horizon. Blencathra will be seen to rise majestically on R of this mountain. An easier route is to follow Route 5 for about half a mile and to then bear R through the boulders for the two summit cairns.

Plate 31 **Route 15** — Great Gable from Sprinkling Tarn

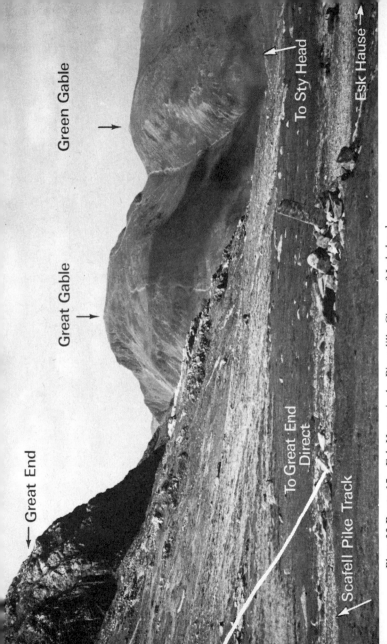

Plate 32 **Route 15**—Esk Hause is the Piccadilly Circus of Lakeland

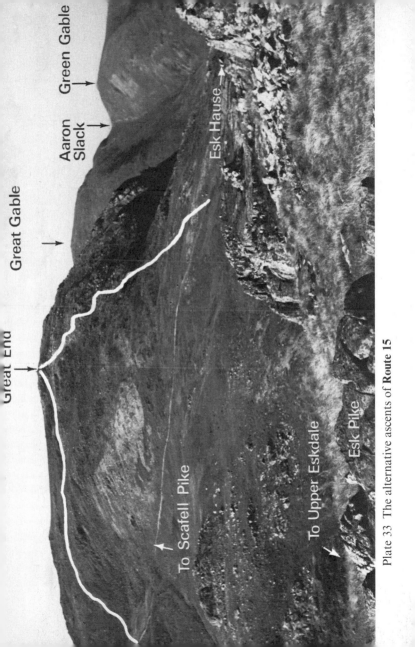

Plate 33 The alternative ascents of **Route 15**

Lingmell

Route 16. From the Lingmell Col. Follow Routes 2, 3, 4 or 9 as far as the col and then bear to the north-west, ascending by the edge of the precipices on the right. The view to the north over Sty Head is magnificent, but the most spectacular prospect is of Great Gable, which is best seen by descending slightly beyond the cairn.

Route 17. From Brackenclose direct. Pass behind the Fell and Rock Climbing Club Hut and cross Lingmell Gill by a small wooden bridge. Keep to the grassy spur of Lingmell all the way, crossing a stone wall about half-way up the mountain. From the top of this spur a broad grassy ridge extends right up to the summit of Lingmell and reveals striking views of Wasdale, Mosedale and Pillar on L, together with a remarkable prospect of Hollowstones and Scafell on R.

Plate 34 **Route 15**—Sprinkling Tarn from the south exit of Central Gully on Great End; the tarn is over 1,000 feet below

Plate 35 **Routes 16** and **17** pass the Lingmell Col

Plate 36 Great Gable from Lingmell, a good viewpoint

The Gable group

Great Gable	2,949 feet	899 metres
Kirkfell	2,631 feet	802 metres
Green Gable	2,603 feet	793 metres
Allen Crags	2,572 feet	784 metres
Glaramara	2,560 feet	780 metres
Brandreth	2,344 feet	714 metres
Grey Knotts	2,287 feet	697 metres
Base Brown	2,120 feet	646 metres
Honister Pass	1,190 feet	363 metres

Great Gable

Route 18. Wasdale, Gavel Neese and the Sphinx Ridge. Leave
Wasdale Green by the lane which passes the church and leads
to the farmstead of Burnthwaite. Take the Sty Head track,
and after crossing the footbridge over the stream coming
down from Beck Head, bear to L up the hillside and pick up
the path which goes through a gate and then keeps to the crest
of Gavel Neese. The ascent of this grassy spur is steep and
arduous and it ultimately gives place to slippery scree, where a
conspicuous erect boulder, known as Moses' Finger,
protrudes from the side of the mountain some distance above.
Bear to R here and follow the Gable Traverse, which passes
below the Napes Ridges, but at Little Hell Gate turn to L up
the scree and hug its retaining wall on R. After a rise of some
200 feet a clearly marked track rises steeply up the crags on R,
and this is the Climbers' Traverse. It crosses the rocky spur
immediately below the Sphinx Rock, which is, however, better
seen some little distance farther on. The Sphinx Gully will be
noticed as the first rift in the crags high up on L. Climb it until
the crest of the ridge is gained and then scramble up this airy
escarpment, which merges with the Arrow Head Arête just

Plate 37 **Routes 18** and **19** on Great Gable, seen from Down in the Dale

Map 2
The Gable Group
Routes 18 to 33

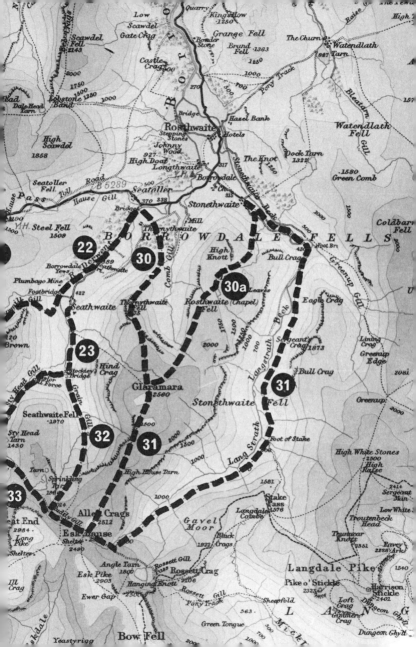

below the Napes summit. This reveals Westmorland Crags, dominated by a large cairn which shields the summit of Gable. While experienced climbers may reach this belvedere by devious routes up the face of the shattered cliff ahead, it is safer for the pedestrian to keep to a track which skirts them on L and so avoid all difficulties.

Considering the importance of Great Gable, the cairn on its summit is scarcely as imposing as it might well be. It has, however, a greater intrinsic interest than any other of the Lakeland summits, for a tablet in the north face of the summit boulder marks the presentation to the National Trust of this and other adjacent peaks in memory of those members of the Fell and Rock Climbing Club who fell in the First World War, 1914–18.

The panorama from this mountain is magnificent and reveals the distant fells in all directions, excepting to the south, where the higher Scafell massif blocks the view and forms a wild and impressive group beyond the Sty Head Pass far below. To R of it, Illgill Head and Yewbarrow together cradle Wastwater backed by the sea in the vicinity of Seascale. Pillar rises superbly above the extensive plateau of Kirkfell to the west, but the High Stile group on its R is not seen to advantage beyond the barren trench of Ennerdale. The Grasmoor Fells, however, afford the most striking prospect to the north-west, with the noble form of Skiddaw rising to their R above Dale Head. Blencathra stands in splendid isolation on the north-eastern horizon, and then the whole of the Helvellyn range occupies the eastern skyline, well above the intervening ridges. The Langdale Pikes are prominent in the south-east beyond the long ridge of Glaramara and the light glints on the waters of Sprinkling Tarn almost immediately below Esk Hause, where the track rising to it from Sty Head may be clearly perceived.

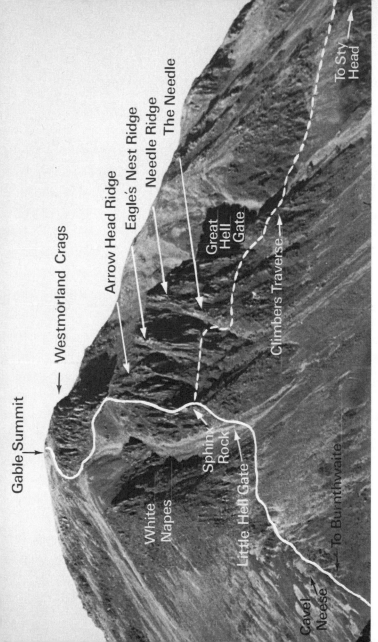

Plate 38 A telephoto shot of **Routes 18** and **25**

Gable Summit

Westmorland Crags

Arrow Head Ridge

Eagle's Nest Ridge

Needle Ridge

The Needle

Great Hell Gate

Climbers Traverse

To Sty Head

White Napes

Sphinx Rock

Little Hell Gate

Cavel Neese

To Burnthwaite

Westmorland's Cairn

Napes Summit

Plate 39 **Route 18**—There are other variations for the rock climber

Plate 40 **Route 18**—Westmorland Cairn from below,
Langdale Pikes in the distance

Route 19. Wasdale, Gavel Neese and Beck Head. Follow
Route 18 to Moses' Finger and then take the rough track
across the scree to L. This emerges at Beck Head near the
smaller of two tarns. Walk on to the small eminence beyond it
on R and then scramble up the steep shoulder on to the
summit, keeping the precipices of Gable Crag well on L.

Route 20. Ennerdale and Windy Gap. The Youth Hostel at the
foot of Black Sail stands at the cross-roads in this western
valley and tracks radiate from it in all directions. Looking to
the south-east, a spur will be observed running up to Green
Gable, with Tongue Beck on L, and the stream descending
from Windy Gap on R. Make for the foot of this escarpment
by crossing the moraine heaps which are a conspicuous
feature hereabouts, and then take a direct line for Windy
Gap, traversing below the crags supporting the summit of
Green Gable. The fine shadowed precipices of Gable Crag rise
on R, and on attaining Windy Gap turn sharp to R and ascend
the track which keeps above them until the summit of the
mountain is reached.

Plate 41 **Route 20** — It's a long walk up Ennerdale to the youth hostel

Route 21. Honister and Green Gable. Pass through the quarry buildings on the south of Honister Hause and ascend the road on R. On reaching level ground bear to L along the prominent track which skirts Grey Knotts and passes to the west of the summit of Brandreth. Hereabouts the views to R along both the Buttermere and Ennerdale valleys are magnificent and reveal the well-known lakes of Buttermere and Crummock Water in the former and of Ennerdale Water in the latter, with the High Stile group of hills rising between them. The track bends to L as far as some small tarns and then ascends by a dilapidated wire fence almost as far as Green Gable. After lingering here to admire the splendid vista down Ennerdale which is dominated by Pillar, descend to Windy Gap and follow Route 20 to the summit of Gable.

Plate 42 **Route 21** — The view from Green Gable

Route 22. Seatoller and Gillercombe. The road to Seathwaite diverges to L just below Seatoller. It crosses a bridge spanning Hause Gill and a mile farther on reaches the bridge over the River Derwent. Go through the two gates on the R of the bridge and follow the path beside the river which passes below the famous Borrowdale Yews to a footbridge at the foot of Sour Milk Gill whose cascades are a prominent feature in wet weather. This is the more beautiful approach but is longer than that which starts under the arch of the farm buildings in Seathwaite. There are well worn tracks on each side of the gill and the more popular one zig-zags up the steep slopes on the L of the stream. Both eventually merge as they enter the spacious hanging valley of Gillercombe, where the Buttress is a conspicuous feature of the crags on the R; it is actually on the south face of Grey Knotts and is one of the local playgrounds for the rock climber. The track keeps to L of the hollow, gradually rising across the flanks of Base Brown to emerge finally on the skyline near the summit of Green Gable. Route 21 then leads to the summit of Great Gable. Buckley's Route keeps to the crest of Base Brown all the way and has the advantage of the views disclosed by this fine fell, but the variation involves the long rough, and continuously steep ascent of some 1,700 feet from Seathwaite.

Plate 43 **Route 22**—Base Brown dominates the approach to Sour Mill Gill

Plate 44 **Route 22**— The ascent on the L of the Gill is the more popular

Route 23. Seathwaite, Sty Head and Aaron Slack. Follow Route 22 to the bridge over the Derwent and continue along the road to the hamlet of Seathwaite. Keep to the broad stony track (which has been admirably repaired by the local authority after the Great Borrowdale flood of August 1966, when it was almost washed away) with the river on R as far as Stockley Bridge, and then after passing through the wall ascend the steep hillside ahead where the track skirts the conifers enclosing Taylor Gill Force. A large cairn here marks the 1,000-feet contour and reveals the many paths across the boggy ground, all of which rise and converge in the deeper confines of the Pass with the stream coming down on R. Cross the footbridge, and as soon as Sty Head Tarn comes into view ahead bear to R over the grassy flanks of the hill and pick up the track by the beck descending from Aaron Slack. Climb up this wild ravine as far as Windy Gap and then turn to L and follow Route 20 to the summit of Gable.

Route 24. Sty Head and the Breast Track. Follow Route 23 to Sty Head Tarn. Pass it on L and at the guide-post turn sharp to R and keep due north-west up the breast of Gable. The track is clearly marked in places but there is no necessity to adhere strictly to it, because the higher slopes converge and terminate at the summit cairn on the mountain.

Taylor Gill Force

Sty Head

Grain Gill

Stockley Bridge

Plate 45 **Routes 23** and **24** take a sharp rise here

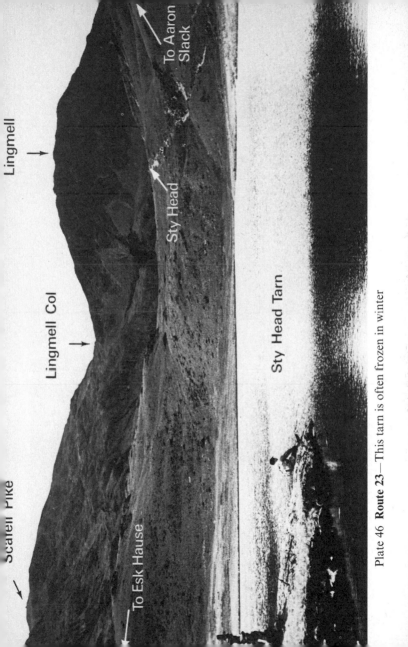

Scafell Pike →

Lingmell →

Lingmell Col →

To Aaron Slack

Sty Head

To Esk Hause

Sty Head Tarn

Plate 46 **Route 23**—This tarn is often frozen in winter

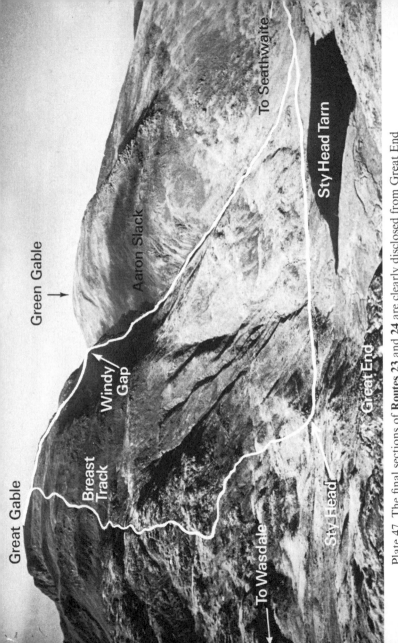

Plate 47 The final sections of **Routes 23** and **24** are clearly disclosed from Great End

Green Gable

Great Gable

Aaron Slack

To Seathwaite

Breast Track

Windy Gap

Sty Head Tarn

Great End

Sty Head

To Wasdale

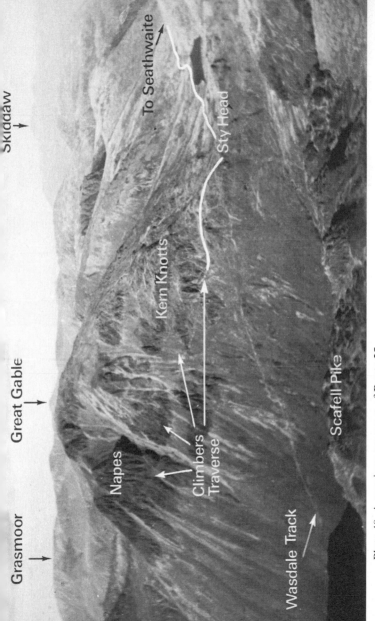

Plate 48 A spacious prospect of **Route 25**

Route 25. Sty Head and the Climbers' Traverse. Follow Route 24 to Sty Head and continue ahead to the large cairn marking the actual summit of the Pass which is to the west of the large boulder. Ascend the small eminence to R of it which discloses the commencement of the Traverse a short distance below, and walk along it into the recess at the foot of Kern Knotts. This imposing crag is unmistakable, and rock climbers may often be seen ascending one or other of the cracks on its seventy-feet face. Scramble down over the maze of large boulders on L, and skirt the Buttress to reach the continuation of the path. This rises across the flanks of Great Gable and reveals splendid views down on L into Wasdale. Some distance higher up it passes another outcrop of rocks where a spring is hidden beneath the overhanging crags on R: this is the last place where a drink may be obtained on this route. Cross the wide exit of Great Hell Gate a few yards ahead and climb the narrow track below Tophet Bastion which rises superbly on R. When it bifurcates keep to the right-hand branch which leads into Needle Gully, because if you follow the left branch it goes below the Napes and joins Route 18 at the exit of Little Hell Gate. Scramble up the slippery bed of the gully as far as the Napes Needle, which stands high up on R, and ascend the rock staircase on L (facing the Needle) which leads to the Dress Circle. This ledge is situated immediately below the gigantic wall supporting the Eagle's Nest Ridge and is well named. Then traverse the ledge carefully round to R, and a few yards farther on squeeze through a narrow gap in the crags which gives access to the Eagle's Nest Gully. There is an awkward step down round the corner on R into it (see plate 52), and the track then passes below the Arrow Head to join Route 18 below the Sphinx Rock.

Innominate Crack

Kern Knotts Crack

Climbers Traverse

Plate 49 The popular rock climbs on Kern Knotts

Eagles Nest Ridge

Abbey Buttress

Needle Ridge

Eagles Nest Gully

Napes Needle

Napes Traverse

Plate 50 The Napes Ridges

Plate 51 **Route 25**—Climbing Napes Needle

Plate 52 On the Napes Traverse

Plate 53 The view from the Sphinx Rock

Grasmoor Wandope Eel Crags Grisdale Pike Hindscarth

Robinson

Fleetwith

Great Gable

Plate 54 North-west from Gable

Plate 55 North-east from Gable

Kirkfell

Route 26. Wasdale and Beck Head. Route 19 may be followed as far as Beck Head, but if a short cut is desired pass through the gate on L of the green strath beyond Burnthwaite and cross some rather boggy ground where a path leads to the stream coming down from Beck Head and ultimately rises to its source at the col. The track to Kirkfell leaves the larger of the two tarns here and zigzags up beside an old wire fence. There are two cairns on the vast plateau, but the best views are obtained from its eastern rim, which reveals an unusual prospect of Great Gable to the east, and by evening lighting a beautiful panorama of the Scafells, which rise above the nearer eminence of Lingmell to the south-east.

Route 27. From Wasdale direct. Leave Wasdale Green by the walled road which passes the Wastwater Hotel and turn L at the guide post to pass behind the 'shop'. Cross the stile near the packhorse bridge and follow the path which rises steeply up the grassy spur of Kirkfell straight ahead, but peters out after the first few hundred feet. Keep to the spur, which finally leads to the higher of the two summit cairns. This is a continuously steep and trying ascent.

Route 28. Wasdale and Black Sail. Follow Route 27 to the gate and then take the path on L which keeps to the stone wall for some distance. It afterwards bears to R and skirts the flanks of Kirkfell as far as Gatherstone Beck, with fine views to L into the spacious hollow of Mosedale. Cross the stream and ascend the steeper track to the top of Gatherstone Head, which discloses its further course swinging round to R to the col on the skyline. This is Black Sail, and from its summit turn sharp to R across the rising ground and scramble up to the shattered crags of Kirkfell which rise high overhead. Follow the sketchy track below the rocks which ultimately leads to the higher of this mountain's two cairns.

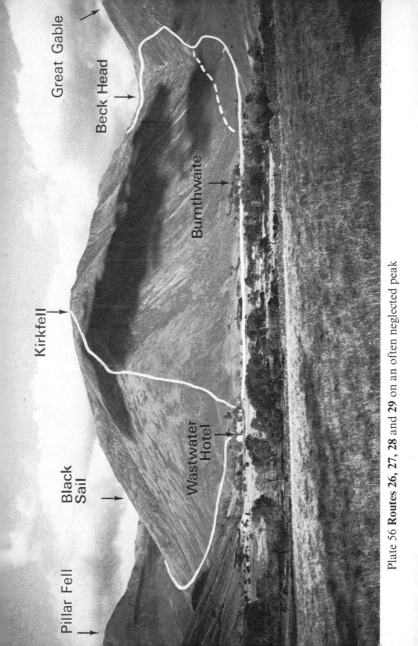

Plate 56 **Routes 26, 27, 28** and **29** on an often neglected peak

Plate 57 **Route 26**— The Scafell Pikes and Lingmell from the summit of Kirkfell

Plate 58 **Route 26**— Retrospect of the Gables

Plate 59 **Route 26**—The tarns and summit cairns on Kirkfell

Route 29. Honister and Moses' Trod. Follow Route 21 as far as Brandreth and then drop down over the grassy flanks of Green Gable. The path known as Moses' Trod is at first rather indistinct, but is quite clearly marked in the vicinity of the stream descending from Windy Gap. Follow it to R, well below Gable Crag on L, where it rises to a small hump which reveals Beck Head with its two tarns just below. Descend to the col and then keep to Route 26 as far as the summit of Kirkfell.

Glaramara

Route 30. Rosthwaite and Thornythwaite Fell. Leave
Rosthwaite by the Seatoller road and walk along it as far as
Mountain View Cottages, which are about a mile beyond the
church and just short of the bridge over the River Derwent. A
stile opposite gives access to the fells, which are at first
sparsely shagged with woods. Pick up the track which rises on
the western side of Comb Gill, and on emerging from the trees
discloses a fine prospect of this gigantic hollow down on L.
The track follows a sinuous course and skirts many a craggy
knoll until it tops the skyline and reveals Gillercombe on the
opposite side of the Seathwaite Valley. It then bears slightly to
L and rises to the cairn on the summit of Thornythwaite Fell.
Here the retrospective view is surprising, for it unfolds a
striking prospect of Honister Crag protruding above the Pass
to the north-west, and also a delightful vista to the north
along the green strath of Borrowdale. The bold summit of
Glaramara appear almost due south, and you cross the
intervening boggy ground in a direct line with it, keeping well
away from the precipitous edge of Comb Gill on the left
which, however, reveals a remarkable view of Doves Nest
Caves opposite. A pleasant scramble leads to the twin cairns
gracing this peak; the near one retrospectively disclosing
Derwentwater and Skiddaw beyond Borrowdale, and the far
one providing a striking prospect of the Langdale Pikes away
to the south-east across the deep trench of Langstrath. A
craggy escarpment on the south partially blocks the panorama
in this direction, but it is worth while to walk over to it for the
view of Great Gable, which rises as a stately giant above the
nearer top of Seathwaite Fell. This belvedere, moreover,
opens up the full-length prospect of the long ridge of
Glaramara to the south and reveals the unexpected
undulations of its topography as far as Allen Crags, together
with the deeply gullied precipitous façade of Great End on R.

Plate 60 **Route 30** ends on a fine Lakeland viewpoint

Gable

Lingmell

Thornythwaite Fell

Johnny Wood

Rosthwaite

Comb Gill

Plate 61 **Route 30**—Looking across Comb Gill to Doves Nest Caves

Plate 62 **Route 30**—Skiddaw and Derwentwater from the summit of Glaramara

Route 30a. Over Rosthwaite Fell. This is a long and circuitous route to Glaramara; it begins at Stonethwaite and should on no account be attempted in dense mist. Follow the cart track in the direction of Langstrath, and after crossing the second stream turn uphill into the trees on R and climb the steep twisted path beside Stanger Gill which in its higher reaches crosses two awkward stone walls below Bull Crag on L before attaining the grassy col. Note the magnificent retrospect of Borrowdale below and then cross a wall and follow Stanger Gill to its source, keeping the several craggy eminences of Rosthwaite Fell on L. Climb the last of them, High Knott, as its cairn opens up a dynamic view of Honister Crag and Seatoller, as well as a splendid vista along Borrowdale to Skiddaw. Then walk due south and ascend Bessyboot which discloses a variety of views in all directions, including Tarn at Leaves which is cradled in a grassy basin at its base and backed by the fine profile of Pike o'Stickle. The route ahead is now clear and the next point of interest is Rosthwaite Cam, to the right of which rises Comb Head, with a glimpse of Glaramara on its R; further to R there is also a good view of Raven Crag on the other side of Comb Gill. Climb the grassy slopes to Rosthwaite Cam and continue ahead to the next eminence of Cam Crag, beyond which there is a lovely tarnlet held in the grip of the hillside above Comb Door. Pass this opening on R and scale Comb Head for the fine backward view of this gloomy hollow, with Doves Nest Caves on R, and then go ahead to the cairn on Glaramara.

Plate 63 **Routes 30a, 31, 108** and **109** from Castle Grag

Plate 64 **Route 30a** — Borrowdale and Stonethwaite from Stanger Gill

Plate 65 **Route 30a**—Skiddaw from Bessyboot—a romantic name!

Pike O'Stikle ⟵

Coniston Fells →

Tarn at Leaves

Plate 66 **Route 30a** passes a tarn that is seldom visited

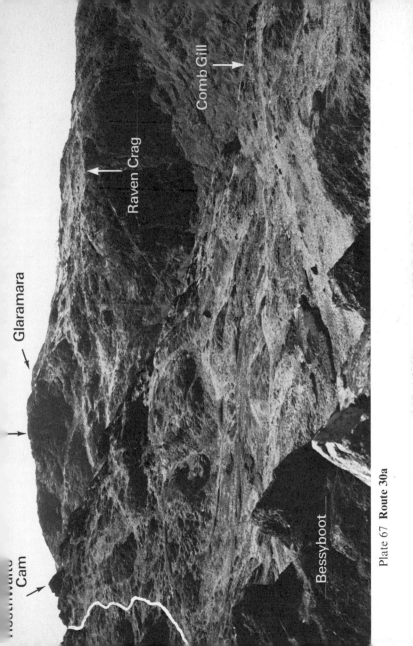

Cam

Glaramara

Raven Crag

Comb Gill

Bessyboot

Plate 67 **Route 30a**

Route 31. Langstrath and Esk Hause. The key to this route is the footbridge over Langstrath Beck at the foot of Eagle Crag, and there are two approaches to it from Rosthwaite. The more common one threads the fields beyond Stonethwaite and joins the stony track at the bend in the river just short of the bridge. The other leaves Rosthwaite by the Hazel Bank bridge and follows the northern banks of Stonethwaite Beck to the new footbridge over Greenup Gill, where a rather indistinct track crosses the fields into Langstrath. Thereafter it is clearly marked as far as the foot of the Stake Pass which rises on L. Cross the bridge here and keep the main stream on R, following it for some two miles to its source just below, but to the east of, Esk Hause. Pick up the Langdale track to the shelter, and then coast round the western flanks of Allen Crags where some small pools lie on a shelf high above Grain Gill. As soon as Glaramara appears to the north, follow the meagre track in this direction which passes between two lovely small tarns where Pike o'Stickle is often mirrored through a gap in the crags.

Route 32. Grain Gill and Esk Hause. Follow Route 23 as far as Stockley Bridge, and after passing through the wall on the other side of the stream turn sharp to L and follow it into Grain Gill. At first the track rises across the flanks of Seathwaite Fell on R, but after crossing Ruddy Gill leave it and keep to its tributary, and come out on the skyline near Esk Hause. Then follow Route 31 to Glaramara.

Route 33. Sty Head and Esk Hause. Follow Route 23 as far as Sty Head, and at the shelter bear to the south-east across the swampy ground and pick up the well-cairned track which skirts the lower slopes of Great End. Pass Sprinkling Tarn, ascend the rising ground with Ruddy Gill on L, and keep straight ahead as far as Esk Hause. Then follow Route 31 to Glaramara.

Plate 68 The Gables and Pillar from Glaramara

Plate 69 **Route 31** — The Langdale Pikes from High House Tarn

The Pillar group

Pillar Fell	2,928 feet	892 metres
Scoatfell	2,760 feet	841 metres
Red Pike	2,707 feet	825 metres
Steeple	2,687 feet	819 metres
Haycock	2,619 feet	798 metres
Seatallan	2,270 feet	692 metres
Looking Stead	2,058 feet	627 metres
Yewbarrow	2,058 feet	627 metres
Black Sail	1,800 feet	549 metres

Pillar

Route 34. Wasdale and the High Level Route. Follow Route 28 to Black Sail, and then turn to L along the ridge leading to Looking Stead. This mountain may, however, be reached more directly from Gatherstone Head by taking a direct line up the fellside. Cross the saddle and bear to the south-west up the ridge rising to Pillar Fell, and at a prominent cairn pick up the High Level Route which diverges to R and provides one of the most spectacular walks in Lakeland. It descends slightly at first and then undulates along the stony shelf which leads to Robinson's Cairn. This discloses the Pillar Rock, one of the most famous climbing grounds in Britain, towards which the track at first descends and then rises to a rocky shelf on L. Ascend this carefully, while noting the splendid conformation of Shamrock, and then scramble round the well-marked rocks encircling the stone shoot above Walker's Gully to Pisgah— the craggy eminence abutting on the hillside to L of High Man, noting on the R the Slab and Notch route to High Man. Here a bold ridge leads up to the skyline on L. Ascend it until the cairn on the summit of the mountain appears ahead.

The panorama from Pillar is extensive, but scarcely

Map 3
The Pillar Group
Routes 34 to 45

impressive, owing to the flattish top of the mountain. The most striking prospect is to the south-east from Great Gable to Scafell; the former appearing above the vast summit of Kirkfell and the latter rising splendidly beyond the deep hollow of Mosedale far below. Red Pike, Scoat Fell and Steeple form a high massive group to the south-west and rather block the distant view, but Ennerdale water may be seen to the west over the long shoulder of the latter. The Grasmoor Hills to the north are largely obscured by the barren craggy slopes of the High Stile range on the other side of Ennerdale. Skiddaw and Blencathra rise on the northern horizon above the western peaks of the Dale Head group, while the Helvellyn range bounds the eastern prospect. The most spectacular view, however, is obtained from the edge of the precipices enclosing Great Doup, slightly to the east of and above the Pillar Rock, where the strangely contorted crags descend in one wild sweep into the depths of Ennerdale, over 2,000 feet below.

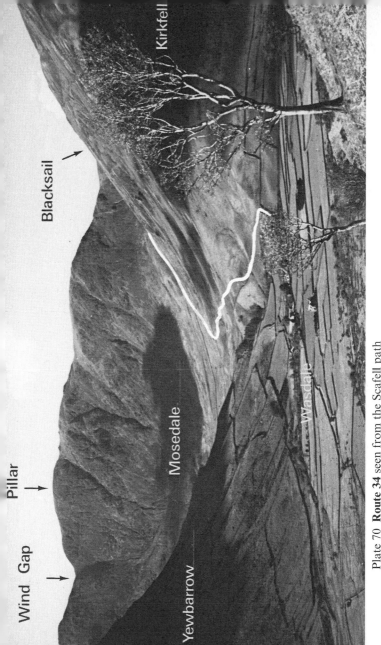

Plate 70 **Route 34** seen from the Scafell path

Plate 71 **Route 34** is clearly revealed from this viewpoint

Plate 72 **Route 34**—Climbers on the High Level Route

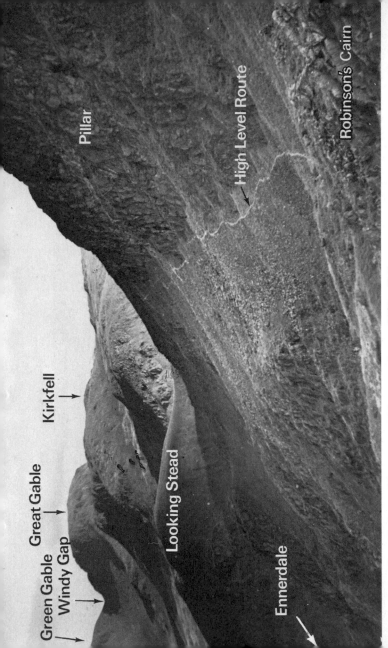

Plate 73 **Route 34** runs across the scree slopes of Pillar Fell

Plate 74 **Route 34**— The east face of Pillar Rock from Robinson's Cairn; the track continues up the shelf on the L

Plate 75 **Route 34**—Shamrock; note the climbers, centre, on Slab and Notch

Plate 76 **Route 34**—Slab and Notch; an easy climb on Shamrock

Plate 77 **Route 34** — High Man from Pisgah

Plate 78 The western face of Pillar Rock

Route 35. Wasdale and Pillar Fell. Follow Route 34 to the cairn marking the commencement of the High Level Route, and then climb up the ridge where a dilapidated wire fence ultimately leads to the summit of Pillar Fell.

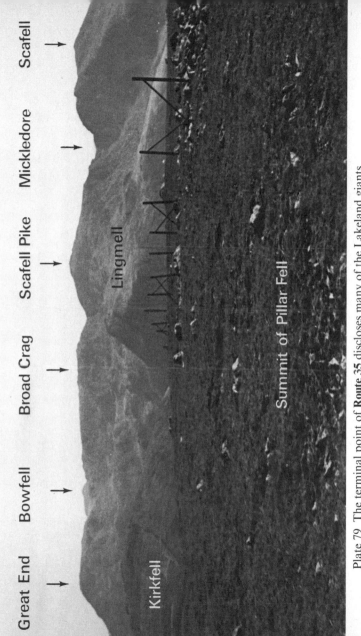

Great End →   Bowfell →   Broad Crag →   Scafell Pike →   Mickledore →   Scafell →

Kirkfell

Lingmell

Summit of Pillar Fell

Plate 79 The terminal point of **Route 35** discloses many of the Lakeland giants

Route 36. Wasdale, Mosedale and Wind Gap. Follow Route 34 until the open fell is reached, then go through a sheepfold and drop down to the stream in Mosedale. Keep this on L for about a mile, thereafter diverging to R, and climb up the rough and steep hillside straight towards the first gap in the skyline on the left of Pillar Fell, taking care not to follow the main stream which rises on Scoat Fell. On reaching Wind Gap, bear to R up the slopes to the summit of the mountain.

Route 37. Wasdale, Dore Head and Red Pike. This route is more generally used to terminate the circuit of the Pillar group, the scree below Dore Head affording a quick means of descent to the valley. Those who wish to ascend it, however, may cross the packhorse bridge behind the Wastwater Hotel, and after passing through a gate leading to the open fell, skirt the northern escarpment of Yewbarrow and climb the steep hillside rising to it. The last few hundred feet are extremely trying, and when the col is attained the craggy slopes on R lead up to the summit cairn on Red Pike. The retrospective view is superb and reveals a wonderful vista along Sty Head where Gable frowns down on one side and Great End rises on the other as a lofty sentinel of the Scafells. The wild rifted aspect of this group as a whole is most impressive. Continuing in a north-westerly direction, the ridge falls slightly and then rises again to Scoat Fell, which discloses Steeple to the north, but the track turns sharp to R and skirts the precipices enclosing the rocky combe, to fall again in Wind Gap, whence the summit of Pillar may be attained by following Route 36.

Route 38. Overbeck and Red Pike. Overbeck Bridge spans the stream which falls into Wastwater near the terminal slopes of the grand southern spur of Yewbarrow. Follow the track on its eastern banks and keep it on L all the way to Dore Head. Then follow Route 37 to Pillar.

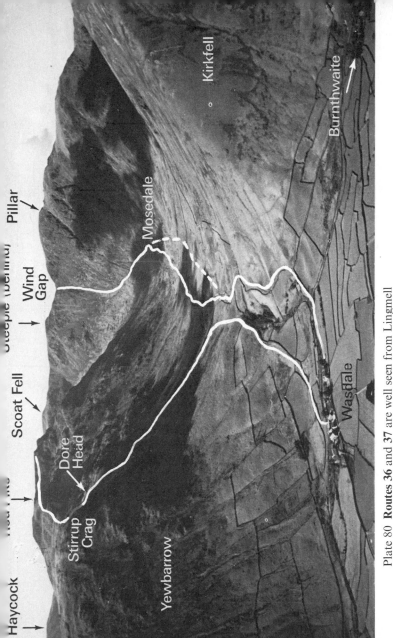

Plate 80 **Routes 36** and **37** are well seen from Lingmell

Haycock · Scoat Fell · Steeple (behind) · Wind Gap · Pillar

Yewbarrow · Stirrup Crag · Dore Head · Mosedale · Wasdale · Kirkfell · Burnthwaite

Route 39. Netherbeck and Scoat Tarn. Netherbeck Bridge is
delightfully situated amid the conifers which grace the
northern shore of Wastwater in the very shadow of Middle
Fell. The stream rises in Scoat Tarn and in its descent form
many pretty cascades, flowing first beneath the craggy slopes
of Seatallan on the west and High Fell on the east, and
thereafter skirting the lower slopes of Middle Fell before
entering the lake. A path ascends by its west bank and affords
a charming ascent of Scoat Fell; the tarn lying below the
saddle connecting it with Red Pike. Route 37 then leads to
Pillar.

Route 40. Ennerdale and Haycock. If you intend to take this
long walk, park your car on the site of the demolished
Anglers' Inn and then proceed along the lake shore to the
Anglers' Crag, whence take a diagonal course across the
flanks of Crag Fell until you strike the tree-girt stream rising
in Black Potts. The alternative is to walk round by Ennerdale
Mill and to then ascend between Crag Fell and Grike until
you reach the same spot. Thereafter, keep to the high ground
above Iron Crag, cross the slight dip to the north of Caw Fell,
and climb by Little Gowder Crag to Haycock. Tewit How
with its small tarn is conspicuous to the north and Seatallan
to the south, while Scoat Tarn appears in the depression to
the east. Steeple and Scoat Fell are now prominent to the
north-east, and the Scafells make a fine skyline above
Yewbarrow to the south-east, but this prospect is not
dissimilar to that already described from Red Pike. The route
becomes more interesting as you advance, because you walk
along the edge of the crags on the Ennerdale side of Scoat Fell
and look down into the wild combes which give birth to Deep
Gill, Low Beck and (beyond Steeple) High Beck. It is well
worth while to scramble along the ridge to Steeple before
joining Route 37 to the summit of Pillar.

Route 41. Gillerthwaite, Haycock and Scoat Fell. The
Ennerdale approaches to the Pillar satellites has been eased by
the opening of the **Nine Becks Walk**, which leaves the Forest
road about one and a half miles from the car park below
Bowness Knott. It drops down to the floor of the dale and
crosses the County Council footbridge on the R below
Gillerthwaite, and later keeps to the R of Woundell Beck to
reach two new footbridges. The first spans Silvercove Beck
and was provided by the Friends of the Lake District, and the
second over Deep Gill was given by the Ramblers'
Association. If you are bound for Haycock, turn R after
crossing the first footbridge and ascend the ridge all the way
to Little Gowder Crag and thence to nearby Haycock, whence
turn L and follow Route 40 to Pillar. If, on the other hand
you are bound for Scoat Fell direct, cross the second
footbridge and turn R for Tewitt How with its adjacent lonely
tarn, then ascend the track to attain the ridge to the west of
your objective and turn L for Pillar.

Plate 81 **Routes 41** and **42**—Friends Bridge

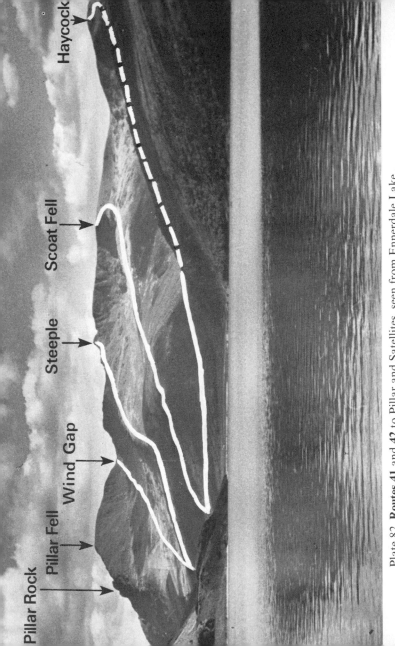

Pillar Rock   Pillar Fell   Wind Gap   Steeple   Scoat Fell   Haycock

Plate 82 **Routes 41** and **42** to Pillar and Satellites, seen from Ennerdale Lake

Route 42. Ennerdale, Steeple and Wind Gap. After crossing the two footbridges continue eastwards along the Becks Walk until you come to Low Beck, whence turn R and climb the track to Steeple, keeping to the edge of Long Crag with Mirklin Cove on the R. Continue along the rocky ridge to Scoat Fell and pick up Route 40 for Pillar. If you are bound for Wind Gap, bear L from Low Beck to reach High Beck, crossing and re-crossing the stream all the way to Wind Gap, whence ascend the ridge on the L for Pillar.

Plate 83 **Routes 41** and **42**—Ramblers Bridge

Plate 84 The key to **Routes 41** and **42**

Plate 85 Steeple—The last stretch of **Route 42**

Plate 86 The final section of **Route 42**, from Steeple, via Scoat Fell

Plate 87 **Route 41** leaves Nine Becks Walk at this point

Route 43. Ennerdale and the Pillar Rock. The Pillar Rock rises majestically to the south-east of Ennerdale and is conspicuous throughout the entire walk up the valley. When immediately below it, cross the River Liza by the Memorial Footbridge and climb the track up the steep and craggy side of the fell into the wild combe below the Rock. Then scramble up to L and join the track to the west of Robinson's Cairn, thereafter keeping to Route 34 to the summit of the mountain.

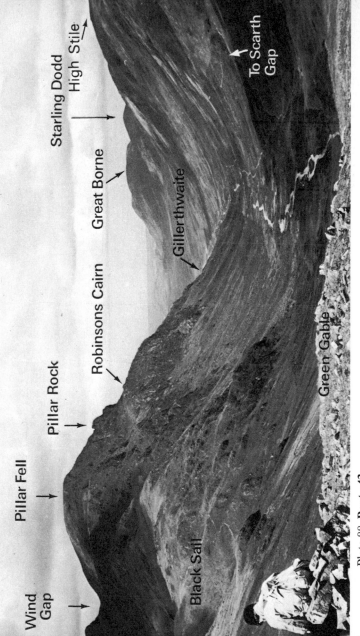

Pillar Fell · Pillar Rock · Robinsons Cairn · Great Borne · Starling Dodd · High Stile

Wind Gap

Black Sail · Gillerthwaite · To Scarth Gap

Green Gable

Plate 88 **Route 43**

Yewbarrow

Route 44. Dore Head and Stirrup Crag. This is the prominent northern tip of Yewbarrow, and its most apt name is only fully appreciated when it is observed from Looking Stead. The quickest way to reach it is by following Route 37 to Dore Head when it towers overhead on L. Steep crags are encountered here and involve some scrambling before the crest of the ridge is attained, whence the cairn on Yewbarrow is reached by walking along the ridge to R.

Route 45. Overbeck and the Great Door. Follow Route 38 as far as the bottom of the southern spur of Yewbarrow. Ascend the track on R which keeps to the western side of the wall, and when the crags are encountered skirt them on L between Overbeck Buttress and Bell Rib. Scramble round the latter on to the crest of the ridge, when the Great Door appears immediately below on the south-eastern face of the mountain. Its vertical retaining walls are conspicuous and provide a spectacular foreground for the view to the east, where the head of Wastwater may be seen far below backed by the magnificent crags of the Scafells. A track goes down the bed of the gully and emerges on steep scree and heather, but its descent is not advisable, since it is easier to continue the walk along the ridge and to descend to the valley by way of Dore Head. The retrospective vista from Yewbarrow of Wastwater stretching away to the south-west is magnificent and reminiscent of one of the smaller Norwegian fiords.

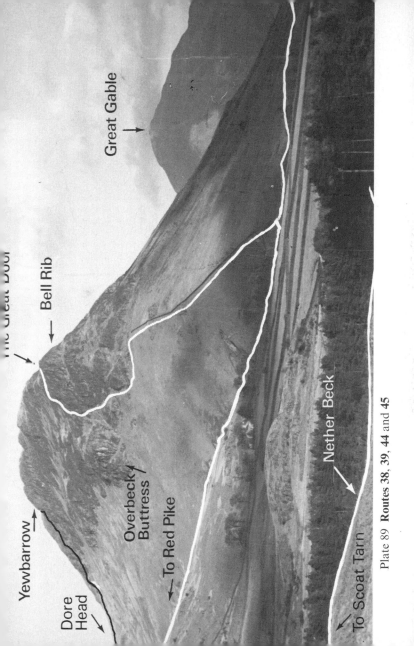

The Great Door

Yewbarrow

Dore Head

Bell Rib

Great Gable

Overbeck Buttress

To Red Pike

Nether Beck

To Scoat Tarn

Plate 89 **Routes 38, 39, 44** and **45**

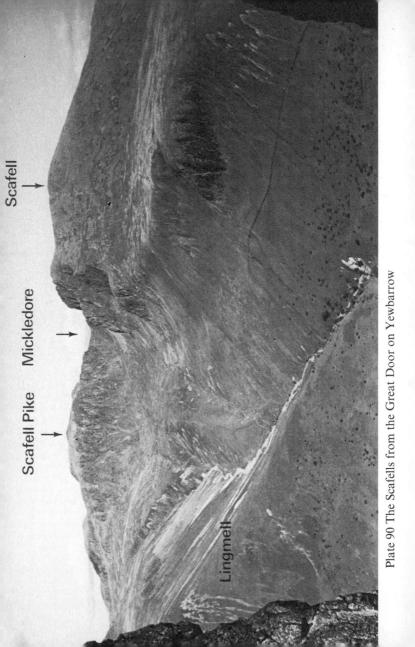

Scafell

Scafell Pike   Mickledore

Lingmell

Plate 90 The Scafells from the Great Door on Yewbarrow

The High Stile group

High Stile	2,643 feet	806 metres
Red Pike	2,479 feet	756 metres
High Crag	2,443 feet	745 metres
Starling Dodd	2,085 feet	636 metres
Great Borne	2,019 feet	615 metres
Haystacks	1,750 feet	533 metres
Scarth Gap	1,400 feet	427 metres
Fleetwith Pike	2,126 feet	648 metres

High Stile

Route 46. Buttermere and Scale Force. Take the cart track to L of the Fish Inn, and cross the fields to Scale Bridge, which is delightfully situated at the foot of the wood-shagged slopes of Red Pike. Turn to R along the stony track which passes near the head of Crummock Water, and in half a mile coasts to L round the flanks of the mountain. The ground is usually wet and boggy, but becomes drier after crossing Scale Beck, which descends in the dip to the south of Mellbreak. As soon as the path rises above the 500-feet contour, Scale Force will be seen in a deep ravine on L, and if the stream is not in spate its cavernous recesses may be entered for a close view of the fall. Now climb up on either side of the beck and adhere to it for about half a mile with Starling Dodd rising ahead. Then bear to L in a south-easterly direction across the long grassy slopes, keeping Ling Combe on L. The tip of Red Pike soon appears ahead and may be attained by a direct ascent. A huge pile of stones marks the summit of this ruddy peak and unfolds an impressive vista to the north where Crummock Water lies cradled far below in the vast basin between Mellbreak on L and Grasmoor on R. This view contrasts admirably with the

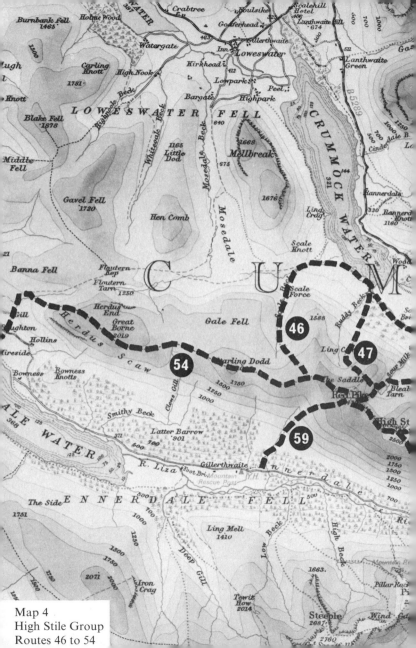

Map 4
High Stile Group
Routes 46 to 54

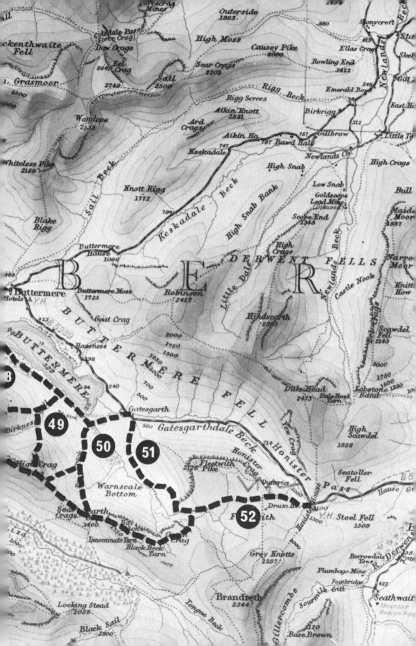

prospect to the south which discloses to advantage the wildly rifted north face of Pillar, together with a glimpse of the Scafells on the distant horizon between it and High Stile. The twin cairns on this, the reigning peak of the group, may be attained by a delightful walk along the edge of the precipices encircling the Combe which reveal Bleaberry Tarn and Buttermere far below backed by the Grasmoor hills away to the north.

The panorama from High Stile is magnificent and particularly so to the south-east, where the whole skyline is resplendent with familiar tops from the Langdale Pikes to Great Gable and the Scafells. The former stand on the horizon above the long shattered ridge ending with High Crag; the Gable rises superbly at the head of Ennerdale far below; while the rifted fronts of the latter completely dominate the scene beyond Looking Stead and Kirkfell. The barren valley immediately below stretches away to the right to end with Ennerdale Water, but the gullied façade of Pillar enclosing it is only seen to advantage by late afternoon light, since at midday it is in shadow. The Grasmoor hills assume a lovely undulating skyline to the north, while the noble forms of Skiddaw and Blencathra close the north-eastern horizon.

Route 47. Buttermere and Ruddy Beck. Follow Route 46 as far as Ruddy Beck, which descends on L and falls into the head waters of Crummock. Climb up through the trees into Ling Combe, keeping the stream on R, and when approaching its source bear to L for the Saddle. Scramble up the slopes of this eminence, which lies immediately to the north of Red Pike, and on reaching the large cairn follow Route 46 to the summit of High Stile.

High Crag

High Stile

Red Pike

Scale Force

Ruddy Beck

Buttermere

Crummock

Lanthwaite Hill

Plate 91 **Routes 46** and **47**—Lanthwaite Hill may be ascended from Scale Hill Hotel

Route 48. Buttermere and Sour Milk Gill. This stream is a conspicuous white ribbon when seen from the village and rises in Bleaberry Tarn to fall into the foot of Buttermere, where its waters enter the river for Crummock. A track from the Fish Inn meanders down to this corner of the lake and crosses the river by a footbridge which gives access to the plantation of larches with Sour Milk Gill descending in a wild ravine on R. The latter may be ascended directly, but the more popular route is by the path rising diagonally through the woods, where the way is obstructed by the trunks of numerous fallen larches. On emerging from the plantation, it zigzags steeply up the overgrown scree, and on reaching a few wind-blown pines bears to R over a shelf to cross Sour Milk Gill well below Bleaberry Tarn. This sheet of water is subsequently passed low down on L as the path rises to the Saddle, whence Route 47 is followed for the summit of the reigning peak.

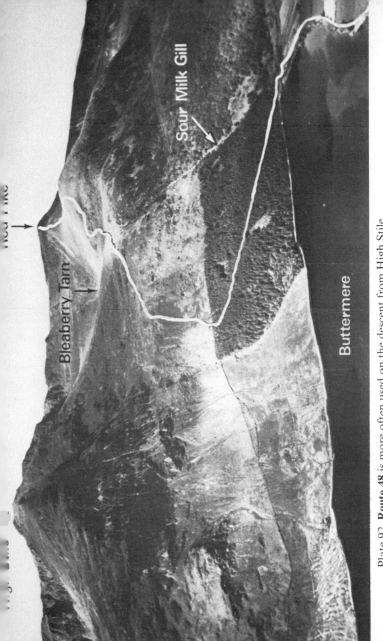

Plate 92 **Route 48** is more often used on the descent from High Stile

Plate 93 **Route 48** — High Stile opens up some fine views

High Stile

Scafell
Pike   Mickledore   Scafell

Pillar

Red
Pike

Plate 94 **Route 48** from Red Pike

Route 49. Buttermere and Birkness Combe. Take Route 48 to
the foot of Buttermere and then keep to the lakeside track
which undulates beneath the larches and discloses many
lovely views of the hills to the north through the foliage. On
emerging from the trees, continue by this path as far as
Birkness Gill and then scale the grassy flanks of High Stile
with the stream on L. A gate in a stone wall gives access to the
vast hollow of Birkness Combe, which is encircled by many
fine but shattered crags. There is no well-marked track, but a
way will be found on R up the barren craggy slopes of High
Stile, whose top is more extensive than may be supposed, the
summit of the mountain being well to the south-west. High
Crag may also be climbed from the floor of the Combe by
first crossing the beck and then making for a conspicuous
ledge high up on L. This leads to the summit with its two
cairns, the farther one revealing a magnificent prospect of the
central Fells with the head of Ennerdale far below. A clearly
marked path keeps to the crest of the ridge connecting High
Crag with High Stile. It skirts the edge of the precipices
overlooking Birkness Combe on R and discloses many of the
striking buttresses and gullies which characterise the enclosing
walls of this great hollow. Grey Crag is the last and most
prominent of the buttresses, and, after passing it, the track
rises amid the great boulders to the cairns crowning High
Stile, which, however, are not perceived until they are almost
reached.

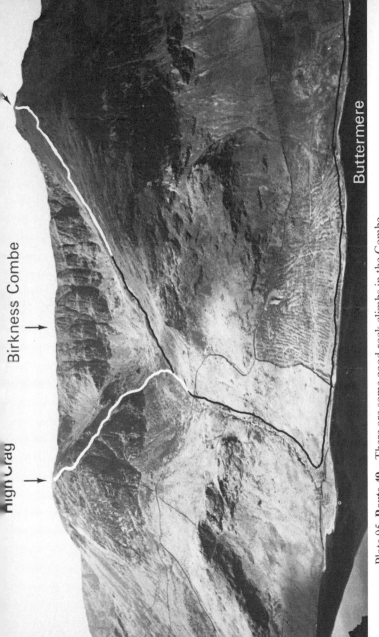

High Crag   Birkness Combe   Buttermere

Plate 95 **Route 49** — There are some good rock climbs in the Combe

Route 50. Buttermere and Scarth Gap. This pass is well known as providing the connecting link between Buttermere and Ennerdale and is crossed when following the usual route to Wasdale. It lies between Haystacks and High Crag and may be attained either by taking Route 49 to Birkness Gill and continuing to the head of Buttermere where the track rises across the hillside on R straight up to Scarth Gap, or by leaving the Honister Road at Gatesgarth and taking the path through the farmstead which leads to the footbridge over the stream in Warnscale Bottom and so joining the other track. High Crag towers overhead on R and may be climbed by several routes, but the more popular one goes up by a stone wall on R just short of the top of the pass. This skirts the base of Seat Crags and then climbs steeply up the grassy slopes of the mountain by a series of well-worn steps which ultimately give place to loose scree before the summit is attained. Route 49 is then followed for the summit of High Stile.

Plate 96 North-east from High Stile

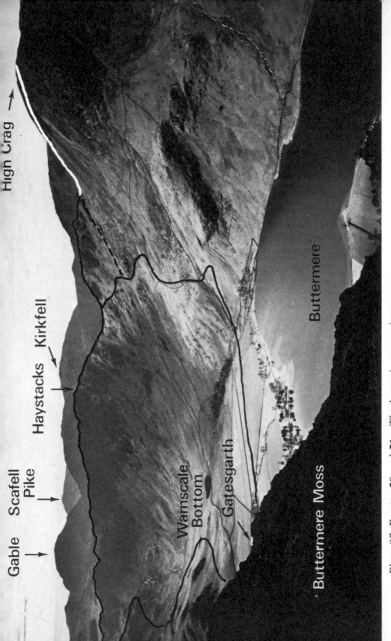

Gable Scafell High Crag →
         Pike

Haystacks Kirkfell

Warnscale
Bottom

Gatesgarth

Buttermere

° Buttermere Moss

Plate 97 **Routes 50** and **51** – The latter is more picturesque

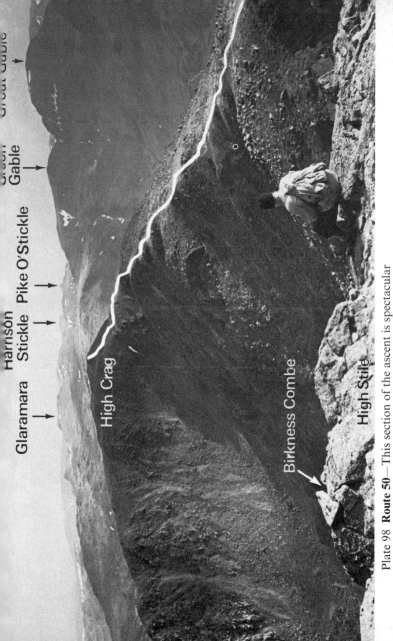

Plate 98 **Route 50**— This section of the ascent is spectacular

Haystacks

Route 51. Warnscale Bottom and Haystacks. Leave the
Honister road beyond Gatesgarth by a path which skirts the
flanks of Fleetwith Pike and rises well above Warnscale
Bottom. When a prominent beck is encountered, follow it to L
and climb up beside it until the old quarry workings are
reached.* Then descend the grassy slopes on R, cross the beck,
and keep to the rim of the precipices overlooking Warnscale
Bottom. The small eminence of Green Crag rises ahead, and
when it has been surmounted Black Beck Tarn appears below.
Descend to its shore and cross the stream issuing from it to
pick up the rough track on R which zigzags up the final slopes
of Haystacks. On attaining the plateau the Innominate Tarn is
at once disclosed, and its setting is the delight of all those who
see it. Walk through the heather on its north-western side and
ascend the rising ground until another small tarn appears
below cradled in solid rock. Go round it to reach the summit
cairn, which reveals High Crag on the other side of Scarth
Gap some 350 feet below. Scramble down the rough slopes
and then follow Route 50 to High Stile.

Route 52. Honister Hause and Haystacks. Walk up the
twisting road on Honister Crag and then bear L along the
disused tram track to the quarry workings. Here join Route
51 for Haystacks and High Stile.

---

* Climbers wishing to take in Fleetwith Pike, for the beautiful vista of the
Buttermere Valley, should ascend its ridge from Gatesgarth and descend from
the cairn to the old quarry workings.

Plate 99 South-east from High Stile—a marvellous panorama

Scafell

Pillar

High Stile

Scafell Pike

Kirkfell

Looking Stead

Gable Great End

Head of Ennerdale

Langdale Pikes

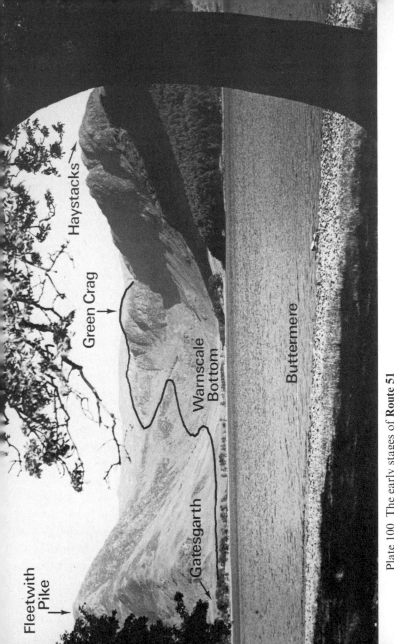

Plate 100 The early stages of **Route 51**

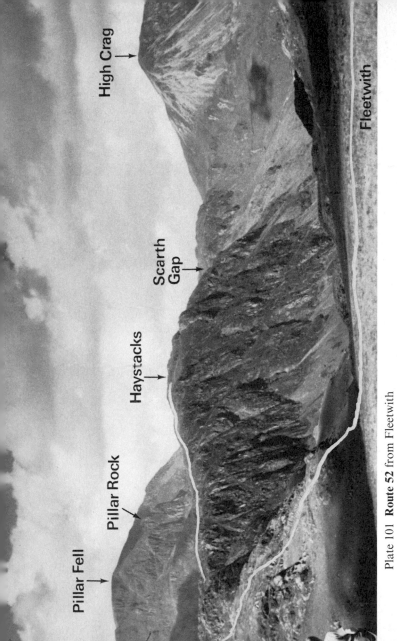

Plate 101 **Route 52** from Fleetwith

Plate 102 **Route 51** — The Gables from Black Beck Tarn

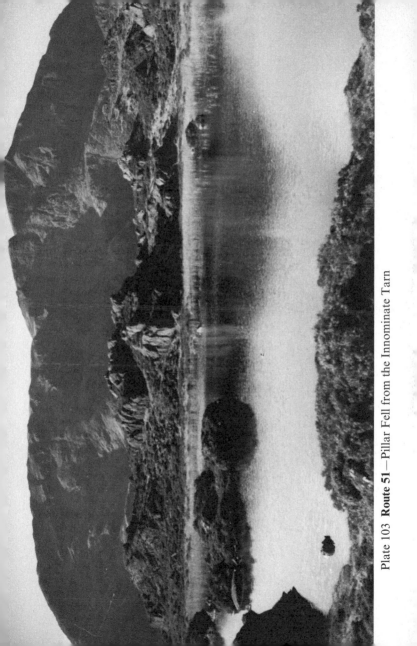

Plate 103 **Route 51**—Pillar Fell from the Innominate Tarn

Plate 104 **Route 51** — The summit tarn of Haystacks. Grasmoor fells in the distance

High Stile

Route 53. Gillerthwaite and Red Pike. A rather indistinct path leaves the Ennerdale pony track by a gate just to the east of Gillerthwaite. It soon peters out, but a way will be found over the rough grassy slopes of Red Pike, first crossing two becks and then bearing to R for the summit of the mountain.

Route 54. Ennerdale and Starling Dodd. Take the route for Floutern Tarn, which leaves Ennerdale Water a few hundred yards to the east of the now demolished Anglers' Inn, and after passing through a gate, rises across a field on L. This gives access to a road by a gate on the left of a cottage, and after passing it and crossing the road walk up a lane which forks on R, but keep straight ahead to emerge on the open fell. Follow the track through several gates with a stream on R, and when the eminence of Floutern Kop appears ahead cross the stream and climb the steep slopes of Herdus End which lead to Great Borne. Then keep to the high ground across the slight depression to Starling Dodd, when the broad ridge rises to the east to end at Red Pike. Follow Route 46 to High Stile.

The Dale Head group

Dale Head	2,473 feet	754 metres
Robinson	2,417 feet	737 metres
Hindscarth	2,385 feet	727 metres
Scawdel Fell	2,143 feet	653 metres
Maiden Moor	1,837 feet	560 metres
Buttermere Moss	1,725 feet	526 metres
Cat Bells	1,482 feet	452 metres
Buttermere Hause	1,096 feet	334 metres

Dale Head

Route 55. Rosthwaite and the Lobstone Band. Enter the narrow walled cart road opposite the post office at Rosthwaite and follow it down to the River Derwent. Turn R, cross the bridge and then L over a footbridge. Follow the R bank of the beck over a stile and ascend a grassy path through the bracken in a direct line with the ravine ahead. Now climb on one side or the other of the stream, and later L up the disused track to the first quarry working on which stands High Rigg Hut. Then climb diagonally on L to the higher slag heaps, where a track leads up to the skyline. Dale Head is now disclosed on the other side of the intervening basin which cradles Dale Head Tarn. Follow the rather wet track round its south side and then strike up the boulder-strewn slopes to the northern façade of the mountain which leads above the shattered cliffs to the cairn on its summit.

The panorama from Dale Head is noteworthy for the vista along Newlands, which stretches away far below and leads the eye over the Vale of Keswick to rest finally upon the noble form of Skiddaw standing on the northern horizon. The deep valley is hemmed in by the precipices of Eel Crags on R and by the steep slopes of Hindscarth on L, but the distant hills on

Plate 105 **Route 55**, seen from Rosthwaite

Map 5
The Dale Head group
Routes 55 to 62

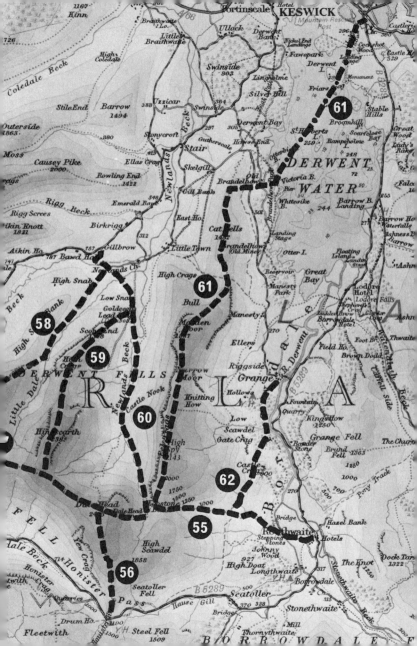

either side are well seen above them. The view to the south is dominated by Gable and the Scafells, which rise above Fleetwith across Honister. They are, however, generally seen in silhouette, unless the climber happens to be on this peak late in the day. The summit ridge narrows considerably to the west of the cairn, and it is hereabouts that the most spectacular views are obtained, since the ground drops away steeply on each side and on the south-west reveals the thin line of Honister Pass descending to Buttermere, which is backed by the High Stile range, seen end-on but in its entirety.

Route 56. Honister direct. A prominent wire fence runs up to the north from the crest of Honister Hause and a track on L leads directly to the cairn on Dale Head. The route is deceptively long, but there are many compensations, not least of which is the grand view of Honister Crag and the deep defile of the Pass on L during most of the ascent.

Hindscarth

To Newlands Beck

Summit of Lobstone Band

Tarn

Plate 106 Final section of **Route 55**

Plate 107 **Route 55** reveals the finest view of Eel Crags

Skiddaw

Blencathra

Dale Head

Eel Crags

Newlands Valley

Plate 108 **Route 55** crosses the narrowest part of the ridge

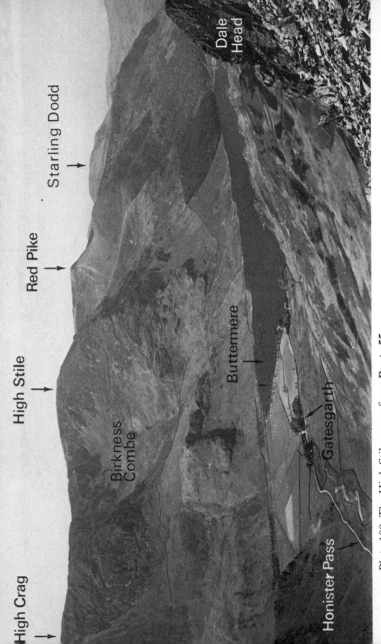

Plate 109 The High Stile range from **Route 55**

Helvellyn Range

Borrowdale

To Dale Head

Summit of Honister

Plate 110 **Route 56**—There is now a car park on the R

Plate 111 **Route 56**—The length of the uphill walk is surprising

Route 57. Buttermere and Robinson. Leave the village by the highway leading to Buttermere Hause, and a short distance from the cross-roads ascend the track on R which rises across the western flanks of Buttermere Moss. It is well marked and bends back to R before topping the skyline. This discloses the vast grassy basin where the path takes a direct line for Robinson across the Moss, but it is advantageous to keep to its edge, which reveals some amazing aspects of Buttermere far below with the High Stile rising majestically in the background. Bear to L when the stream descending to Hassness is encountered and make direct for the summit of Robinson. While this is a somewhat circuitous route for those in a hurry, the cairn discloses a striking prospect round the northern arc from Grasmoor to Blencathra, much of which is not seen if the actual top is avoided. Turn back to the south and descend over the shaly top as far as the wire fence which meanders over the ups and downs of Hindscarth to rise finally to the cairn on Dale Head. The whole walk over this ridge is easy going and rich in marvellous prospects to the right, yielding a remarkable aspect of Pillar which rises superbly beyond Haystacks and Scarth Gap to the south-west.

Route 58. Newlands and Robinson. Take the road going west from Newlands Church to Gillbrow and leave it by the track diverging to L for High Snab. Continue along the flanks of High Snab Bank with the stream coming down from Little Dale on L and in just over a mile climb the slopes on R and make for the northern escarpment of Robinson. Keep the crags on R and continue the ascent in a south-westerly direction until the summit cairn appears on the skyline ahead. Then follow Route 57 to Dale Head.

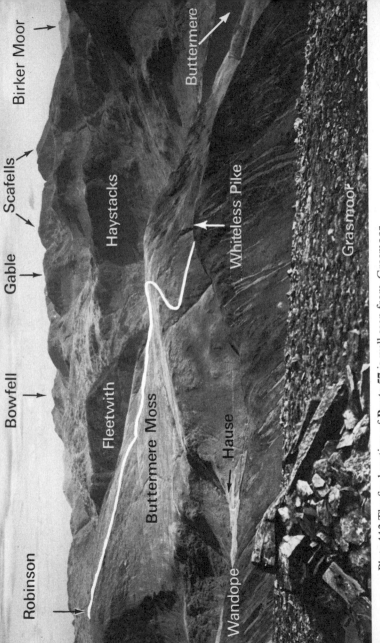

Plate 112 The final section of **Route 57** is well seen from Grasmoor

Plate 113 West from Robinson

Route 59. Newlands and Hindscarth. Take the left fork at
Newlands Church and proceed due south to the foot of Scope
End. Scale the slopes, which rise sharply, and keep to the crest
of the ridge as far as High Crags, when Hindscarth will be
seen ahead. Attain and traverse its summit ridge, finally
bearing to L for the wire fence running up to Dale Head. This
route reveals a striking aspect of the long line of shattered
cliffs known as Eel Crags which stretch from Maiden Moor
nearly as far as Dale Head Tarn and form the dramatic
eastern wall of the Newlands Valley.

Route 60. Newlands Beck and Dale Head Tarn. Follow Route
59 to the old lead mines but thereafter continue due south
until Newlands Beck is encountered. Advance beside it into
the deep recesses of the valley, and when below Scawdel Fell
pick up the track which rises on L across the scree, to finally
emerge at Dale Head Tarn. Then follow Route 55 to the
summit of the reigning peak of the group. There is an
alternative approach from Little Town, whence a grassy cart
road follows an almost level course across the flanks of
Maiden Moor as far as Castle Nook. The waterfall beyond is
worthy of note and lies beside the Beck.

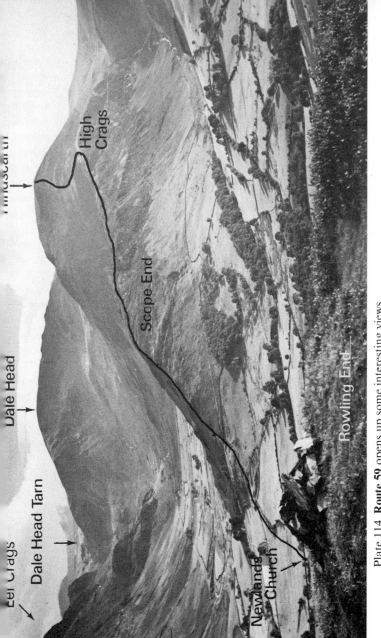

Plate 114 **Route 59** opens up some interesting views

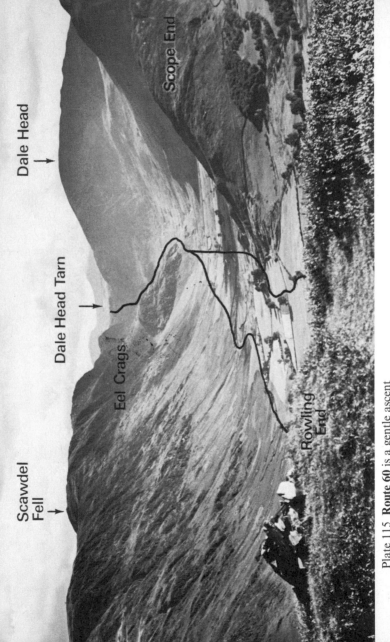

Scawdel
Fell

Dale Head Tarn

Dale Head

Eel Crags

Scope End

Rowling End

Plate 115 **Route 60** is a gentle ascent

Scawdel Fell Maiden Moor Cat Bells

Knitting
How

Friar's Crag

Derwent Water

Plate 116 The ups and downs of **Route 61**

Route 61. Keswick and Cat Bells. A most enjoyable prelude to this walk is to sail across Derwentwater and disembark at the first pier in Brandlehow Park. Then ascend to the road and walk to R until the track on L zigzags up the grassy northern escarpment of Cat Bells. As height is gained, so the views of the lovely lake below increase in grandeur and reveal more clearly its beautiful setting. The track descends sharply to the south of this well-known eminence and cuts across the Newlands–Grange path which descends direct to Manesty low down on L. It continues due south and you ascend its sinuous uphill course over the grassy top of Maiden Moor, where you will then go over to the edge of the precipices on R and follow them all the way to Scawdel Fell, making only one digression to L to stand by the cairn on Knitting How, which discloses a most magnificent aspect of Derwentwater. Keep to the crest of Eel Crags, and while noting the fine prospect of Dale Head do not forget the view to the north-west, where the Grasmoor Hills, and especially Grisedale Pike, form a grand serrated skyline. Then wander down to Dale Head Tarn and pick up Route 55 to the summit of its parent peak.

Route 62. Grange and Castle Crag. Leave Grange by the cart road which turns to L beyond the cottages and threads the trees below Gate Crag. It rises to pass through the narrow defile between Castle Crag on the east and the precipitous face of Scawdel Fell on the west, ultimately petering out at the quarries in the Lobstone Band. A cairn stands on its crest, where a path diverges to L and after crossing a stile and passing through a disused quarry emerges on the summit of Castle Crag.

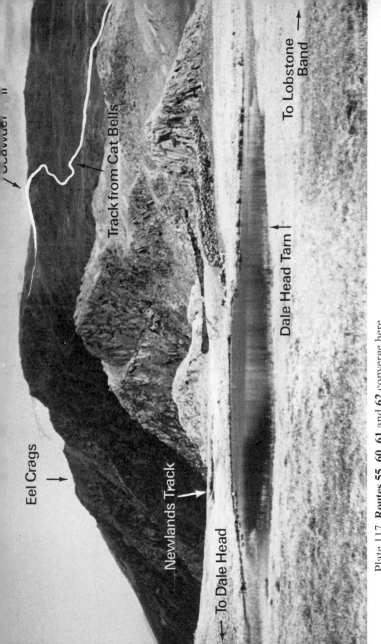

Eel Crags →

Track from Cat Bells

Newlands Track →

← To Dale Head

Dale Head Tarn ↑

To Lobstone Band →

Plate 117 **Routes 55, 60, 61** and **62** converge here

The Grasmoor group

Grasmoor	2,791 feet	851 metres
Eel Crag	2,749 feet	838 metres
Grisedale Pike	2,593 feet	790 metres
Wandope	2,533 feet	772 metres
Hobcarton Pike	2,525 feet	770 metres
Sail	2,500 feet	762 metres
Whiteside	2,317 feet	706 metres
Scar Crags	2,205 feet	672 metres
Whiteless Pike	2,159 feet	658 metres
Causey Pike	2,000 feet	610 metres
Rowling End	1,422 feet	433 metres
Kinn	1,167 feet	356 metres

Grasmoor

Route 63. Braithwaite and Grisedale Pike. Leave the village by the road to Whinlatter, and at the first bend strike up the slopes of Kinn on L. This path rises directly from the car park and involves some collar work for the first 700 feet of "steps" which are rather like a long staircase. In dry weather they may be negotiated easily, but after rain they can be muddy, slippery and difficult. However, there is an alternative at an easier gradient; it starts after a five minute walk up the Pass, opposite the gated entrance to Greengarth, and as a grassy path rises gently through the bracken to Three Stones where it joins the more direct route. The lawn-like path now goes along the top of this eminence with a vast plantation of conifers on R. Grisedale Pike rises ahead with its prominent eastern arête seen end-on and the track takes an oblique line through the prolific growth of heather and bilberries to attain its crest just below the summit. During the first part of the climb the retrospective views towards Derwentwater are very

Causey Pike   Sail   Eel Crags   Grasmoor   Grisedale Pike

Coledale Pass

Kinn

Braithwaite

Portinscale

Latrigg

Keswick

Plate 118   A distant view of the first section of **Route 63**

Map 6
The Grasmoor group
Routes 63 to 67

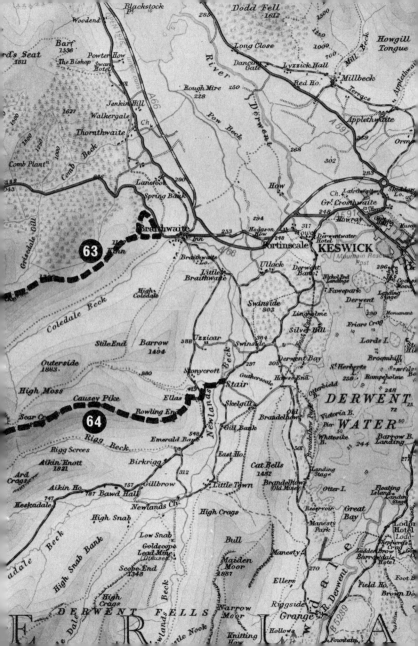

beautiful, but the almost parallel ridge above Causey Pike shuts out the scene to the south. From the summit of the mountain the panorama is more extensive round the whole arc, excepting to the south-west, where the great bulk of Grasmoor obscures the distant view. By far the most striking prospect, however, is to the west, where the shattered crags of Hobcarton Pike present a savage appearance, falling precipitously into the vast intervening combe.

Descend by the track which follows a dilapidated stone wall and skirts this hollow, diverging to R to observe the scene from the summit of the crags. Then turn back to L across Sand Hill and traverse the col known as the Coledale Pass, which is some distance below. Daw Crags rise steeply to the south, but keep them on L and make for the stream coming down from the dip between Eel Crags on L and Grasmoor on R. During this part of the ascent the surprisingly broken flanks of the latter will be noticed. Bear to R up the grassy slopes and follow the edge of these precipices, which form the northern boundary of its extensive grassy summit plateau. Gaskell Gill is hidden by the lower declivities of Brackenthwaite Fell and is frowned upon on the north by the seamed flanks of Whiteside. When the ground to the west begins to fall, turn to L across the plateau and advance to the third cairn, which overlooks the foot of Crummock and discloses a bird's-eye view of Loweswater farther to the west. Then turn to L again and follow the edge of the southern precipices of the mountain to the second and highest cairn.

The panorama from Grasmoor is undoubtedly one of the finest in Lakeland, but to see it at its best it must be observed in the late afternoon of a favourable summer day. At that time the sun is well round to the west when all the peaks engirdling the vast horizon from Skiddaw to Scafell are viewed by the most favourable lighting, and especially so the Central Fells, which are in silhouette earlier in the day. The succeeding ridges to the east afford a wonderful vista and are backed by the Helvellyn range where Catchedicam is a conspicuous cone to L of the reigning peak. The Langdale

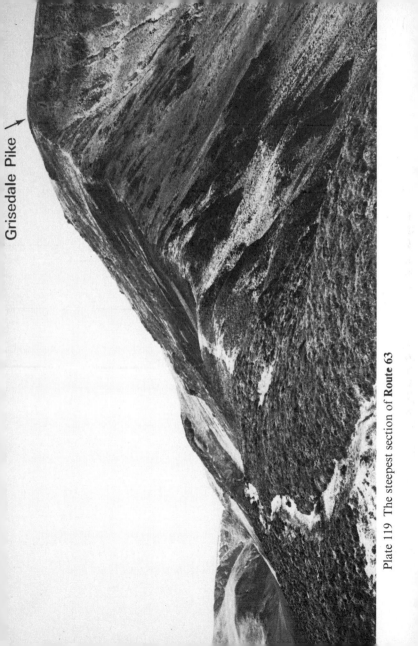

Grisedale Pike

Plate 119 The steepest section of **Route 63**

Pikes are prominent in the south-west, the tip of Pike o' Stickle appearing just to L of the summit of Glaramara. The eye will, however, be attracted by the magnificent array of familiar tops to the south which stretch across the skyline from Wetherlam on L, over Bowfell and Gable, to Scafell on R. The higher cairn on Kirkfell is then disclosed together with a glimpse of the distant hummocks of Birker Moor, seen in the gap between it and Pillar, which rises majestically above the serrated ridge of the High Stile range. Fleetwith and Haystacks look mere insignificant excrescences in the middle distance beyond Buttermere Moss and Whiteless Pike, whose southern escarpments sink down gracefully to Buttermere and Crummock cradled in the narrow valley far below.

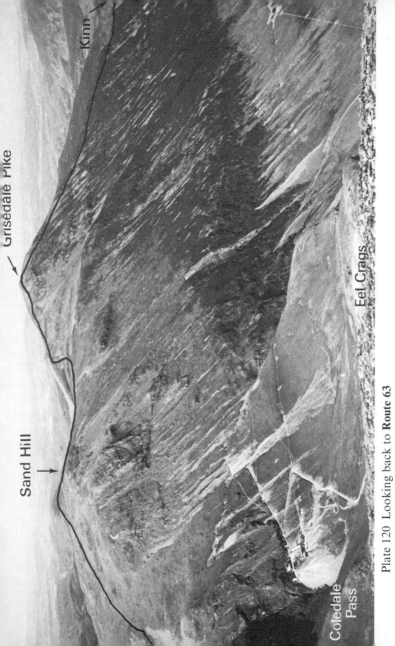

Kinn

Grisedale Pike

Sand Hill

Coledale Pass

Eel Crags

Plate 120 Looking back to **Route 63**

Route 64. Stair and Causey Pike. Leave Stair by the
Buttermere road, and at its junction with the highway coming
south from Braithwaite strike up the obvious path on R which
rises obliquely across the northern flanks of Rowling End.
This is the most direct approach to Sleet Hause which lies at
the foot of the sharp arête to Causey Pike, but it may be
reached by a more revealing route which diverges to the L at
Ellas Crag and on attaining Rowling End traverses the full
length of the broad ridge with superb prospects on the L of
Newlands and its enclosing fells. Now ascend the track which
goes straight up the ridge of Causey Pike, scrambling up its
craggy thimble-shaped top to attain the summit cairn. This
reveals the continuation of the track, which keeps to the edge
of Scar Crags and then zigzags up the long grassy slopes of
Sail. Cross the fine little ridge which joins it with Eel Crags
and walk due west across its shaly top until a small pool is
disclosed in the grassy dip below Grasmoor. Descend to it and
then bear to the north-west to pick up Route 63. This ascent
is superior to the latter because it affords some grand
prospects of the Dale Head group and especially of the deep
valleys which penetrate it.

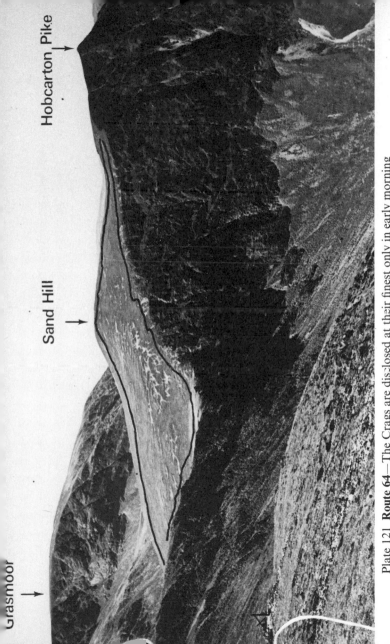

Grasmoor   Sand Hill   Hobcarton Pike

Plate 121 **Route 64**—The Crags are disclosed at their finest only in early morning

Rowling End Sleet Hause Causey Pike

Plate 122 **Route 64** starts here

To Rowling End

To Stair

Plate 123 **Route 64** from Sleet Hause ascends the arête to Causey Pike

Sail   Eel Crags   Grasmoor   Coledale Pass

Scar Crags

Causey Pike

Plate 124 Causey Pike opens up the long section of **Route 64**

Plate 125 Retrospect of **Route 64**

Route 65. Buttermere and Wandope. The usual route leaves the
road to Crummock at Crag Houses and rises across the grassy
slopes of Blake Rigg, but a pleasanter variation is to pass
through the gate opposite the Bridge Hotel and follow Sail
Beck beneath the leafy trees for some distance before
diverging to L to climb it. The track goes to L of this top and
emerges on the grassy col immediately below Whiteless Pike.
The ascent now steepens considerably and reveals increasingly
wide retrospective vistas to the south. The ridge connecting
the summit with Wandope is narrow with magnificent views
down on either side. The cairn on the latter discloses the col
to the north between Grasmoor and Eel Crags, where Route
64 is picked up for the reigning peak.

Plate 126 **Route 65** makes a pleasant afternoon ascent

Eel Crags → Wandope → Grasmoor →

Whiteless Pike

Sail Beck

High Stile

Plate 127 The final section of **Route 65**, seen from High Stile

Grasmoor 1st Cairn

Wandope

Plate 128 A close view of the last rise on **Route 65**

Route 66. Lanthwaite Green and Gaskell Gill. This hamlet stands in the very shadow of the great shattered western façade of Grasmoor, an aspect of the mountain that affords some surprise to the newcomer. Whiteside rises to the north and a wild ravine separates them, through which Gaskell Gill threads its way to ultimately fall into the River Cocker beyond Brackenthwaite. Park your car on Lanthwaite Green or in the nearby enclosure and walk down the cart track to a footbridge over the stream or when the water is low cross the Stepping Stones nearby. Then turn R and keep to the path on its northern banks as far as the Coledale Pass, whence Route 63 leads to the summit of the mountain.

Route 67. Whiteside and Hobcarton Pike. The western escarpment of Whiteside is steep and craggy, so that the track from Brackenthwaite keeps to L and bends round to R near the top for the summit cairn. The ridge is narrow and discloses some extensive views to the north over the Solway Firth to the Scottish hills. It drops slightly before Hobcarton Pike is reached, where Route 63 is joined for Grasmoor.

A more interesting ascent that will appeal to the energetic fell walker is to follow Route 66 to the first bend in the ravine and to then bear L and climb the eminence of Whin Ben. Thence keep to the crest of the ridge all the way to Whiteside, with spectacular views down into Gaskell Gill on the R. After passing the summit cairn continue to Sand Hill and then descend to the Coledale Pass to pick up Route 63 for the summit of Grasmoor.

Plate 129 **Route 66** affords a long walk to Coledale Pass

Whiteside

Grasmoor

Gaskell Gill

Plate 130 **Route 67** yields a spectacular view of Whiteside

Coniston Old Man — Wetherlam — Bowfell — Esk Pike — Great End — Gable — Scafell Pike — Scafell — Kirkfell

Buttermere Moss

Grasmoor

Plate 131 On a clear afternoon this is the ultimate reward of **Route 67**

Skiddaw and Blencathra

Skiddaw	3,054 feet	931 metres
Low Man	2,837 feet	865 metres
Carl Side	2,400 feet	732 metres
Blencathra	2,847 feet	868 metres

Skiddaw

Route 68. Latrigg and Jenkin Hill. Leave Keswick by the road to the R of the station and then walk to L as far as the second turning, where Spoony Green Lane diverges to R. Follow this cart track to the cottages on L and then ascend the well-worn path skirting the western flanks of Latrigg. Most of the trees on the higher declivities have been felled, but keep to the path which rises to the remaining larch wood, and at the end of it turn sharp to R and follow the zigzags to its summit. This divergence from the direct route to Skiddaw is well worth while because it unfolds some magnificent prospects to the south and west which are in fact superior to those from the parent mountain. Walk along the crest of Latrigg and when Blencathra is fully revealed to the east, turn to L and descend by a wire fence which drops down the hillside to the main track. Turn to R and go over a stile; then bear to L at the foot of Jenkin Hill, which clearly displays the steepest section of the ascent. Keep the wire fence on L and after passing the ruined refreshment hut climb with the wall on R as far as the cairn on the 2,000-feet contour; then bear to L and follow the path in a direct line with Low Man. Most pedestrians traverse this subsidiary top, which is spoilt by a cairn consisting of old pieces of iron fencing. Descend again to the main path which keeps to the edge of the vast hollow on L and eventually reaches the south cairn on the long summit ridge. Turn to R along it to attain the highest

Plate 132 **Routes 68** and **69** start from Keswick

Dodd Fell

Ullock Pike

Carl Side

Skiddaw

Low Main

Jenkin Hill

Latrigg

Spoony Green lane

Millbeck

Keswick

Castle Head

Map 7
Skiddaw and Blencathra
Routes 68 to 72

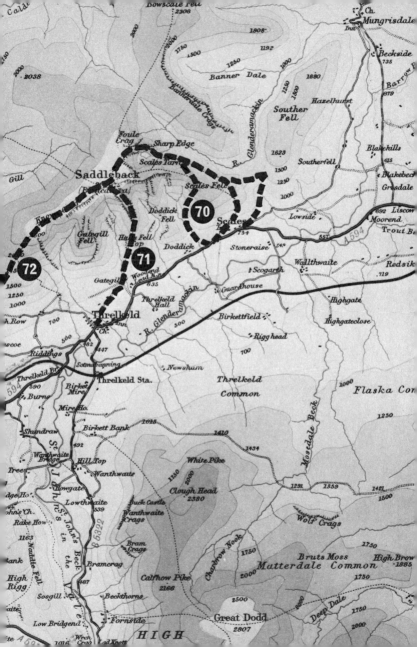

cairn overlooking the foot of Bassenthwaite, but this is not such a good viewpoint as the first cairn, which discloses the immense panorama stretching from Helvellyn in the south-east to Grasmoor in the west. Derwentwater is the most conspicuous feature far below which in the sunlight ripples away into the Jaws of Borrowdale and is backed by the majestic fronts of Glaramara and the Central Fells.

Route 69. Millbeck and Carl Side. Millbeck is more famous for the Terrace Walk connecting it with Applethwaite than as the starting-point for the ascent of Skiddaw. The chief merit of the Terrace is its vista to the south over Derwentwater, but its low elevation does not do justice to the scene. This is, however, advantageously viewed from Carl Side, which dominates the hamlet and reveals the lake and dale from approximately the same angle, it being in a direct line with the maximum length of both Derwentwater and Borrowdale. To attain it leave the road at Millbeck where it crosses the stream and keep to its west bank for a short distance. Then strike up the spur of Carl Side, which rises immediately to R of the plantations on Dodd Fell. Ascend its crest all the way, and at the cairn bear to R for the southern end of the summit ridge of Skiddaw.

Low Man

Jenkin Hill

Ruined hut

Plate 133 **Route 68** is a long plod

Plate 134 South-western prospect from **Route 68**

Robinson

Hindscarth

Dale Head

Cat Bells

Jaws of Borrowdale

Derwentwater

Keswick

Latrigg

Path from Keswick

To Jenkin Hill

Blencathra

Lakeland visitors usually walk up from Keswick to Castlerigg
to see the Druid's Circle which stands in a bleak situation
some 700 feet above sea level. Oval in shape, it has a diameter
of about one hundred feet and commands some fine views of
the surrounding fells. Most imposing of these is Blencathra,
with its ridges rising to the summit of Halls Fell Top. The
view in the reverse direction from this coign of vantage reveals
the Grasmoor Fells, from Causey Pike to Grisedale Pike. The
various routes to the summit of Blencathra, known also as
Saddleback, are as follows:

Route 70. Scales and Sharp Edge. There are two approaches to
Sharp Edge from Scales: the first is circuitous, but at an easy
gradient; the second is direct and very steep, but reveals the
most spectacular aspect of the lateral southern spurs of
Saddleback. The key to the former route is the well-trodden
path running parallel to, but well above and on the west side
of the River Glenderamackin. It may be reached from Scales
by one of the three following variations: (a) Take the narrow
road for Mungrisedale which branches to the left from the
Penrith road just beyond the inn. Some short distance ahead,
a gate on L gives access to a depression in the hillside known
as Mousthwaite Comb, where a track meanders through the
bracken up the eastern flanks of Scales Fell and later bears R
to emerge on a little col overlooking the river. At this point
turn sharp L and follow the direct and almost level path for
Sharp Edge. (b) Pass through the farmyard to the west of the
inn and make for the gate in the L top corner of a steep
pasture. Thence two paths on the R, one above the other,
ascend the southern flanks of Scales Fell and on reaching
higher ground they merge and swing round its eastern slopes
to join the other path some distance from the col. On reaching
Scales Beck, cross it and climb beside the stream to the Tarn,
whence bear R up the grassy slopes to attain the eastern
terminus of Sharp Edge. The crest of this narrow ridge may

be traversed by those with a steady head and good balance, but it is easier and safer to keep to the R just below it until the *mauvais pas* is reached. This is a short hiatus in the ridge and to cross it requires courage and a bold step or two to gain the path which continues to the foot of the inclined slabs that form the steep escarpment of Foule Crag. Great care is necessary here, especially after rain when the slabs are wet and slippery, but a little chimney on the R facilitates progress. On gaining the summit plateau, which is expansive and forms the conspicuous Saddle, bear to L for the cairn on Hall's Fell Top. For the latter route, go through the first farmstead in Scales and climb the steep southern slopes of Scales Fell, keeping well to L to overlook the lower Doddick Fell. Diverge to R near the top, when Scales Tarn will be seen below; descend to it and cross the outflow to join the former route to the summit.

The panorama from Blencathra is one of the most extensive and unobstructed in Lakeland. The whole range of High Street is laid bare to the south-east and ends with the shapely cone of Ill Bell. Helvellyn is seen end-on to the south and is thus uninteresting, but the vista down the Vale of St. John with Thirlmere beyond is a delight and more than compensates for its tameness. The lower half of Derwentwater is revealed in the south-west and to R of Walla Crag, while the whole skyline beyond is resplendent with the familiar peaks of the Central Fells, together with the Dale Head and Grasmoor Groups. Skiddaw appears as a shapeless mass to the west and the vast solitudes of its Forest stretch away into the dim distance to the north.

Route 71. Threlkeld and Hall's Fell Top. About half a mile to the north-east of the village a lane on L goes to Gategill, which is situated immediately below Hall's Fell Top. Pass the cottages on R and keep the stream on L. On gaining the open fell, strike straight up the spur, which is at first grassy, then thickly covered with heather, until finally a splendid narrow rock arête leads up to the summit of the mountain.

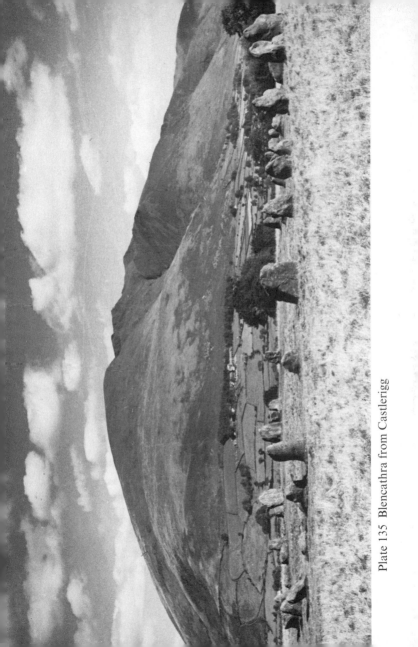

Plate 135 Blencathra from Castlerigg

Plate 136 The Grasmoor Fells from the Druid's Circle

Hall's Fell Top   Saddle   Foule Crag   Sharp Edge

Scales Fell

Col

Scales

Plate 137 Blencathra from the east—**Route 70** and variations

Foule Crag — Sharp Edge

Plate 138 **Route 70** crosses Sharp Edge above Scales Tarn

Plate 139 **Route 71** involves a continuous steepness

Knowe Crags

Gategill Fell

Halls Fell Top

Gategill

Threlkeld

Route 72. Keswick and the River Greta. Take the Penrith road, and after passing under the railway turn to L across a bridge spanning the River Greta. Bear to R and follow the path which threads the lovely woods fringing the northern banks of the stream for a distance of about two miles. Cross Glenderaterra Beck by another bridge and ascend the track in a north-easterly direction with the wide grassy slopes of Saddleback ahead. Breast these long declivities until Knowe Crags are attained and then walk along the ridge which sweeps round high above the fine southern spurs of the mountain until the summit cairn is reached. This route is much finer in the reverse direction when the western panorama is spread out at one's feet during the whole of the descent.

Blencathra summit

Halls Fell Top

Gategill Fell

St. John's Vale

To Keswick

Plate 140 **Route 72** is the best descent for views

Blencathra
summit

Halls Fell Top

Doddick
Fell

Scales Fell

Plate 141 The Blencathra ridges in Alpine conditions

← To Halls Fell Top

Foule Crag

Plate 142 **Route 70** crosses Sharp Edge

Plate 143 **Route 70** — Climbers crossing Sharp Edge in dense mist

The Helvellyn group

Helvellyn	3,116 feet	949 metres
Raise	2,889 feet	881 metres
Dollywaggon Pike	2,810 feet	856 metres
Great Dodd	2,807 feet	855 metres
Stybarrow Dodd	2,756 feet	840 metres
Sticks Pass	2,420 feet	738 metres
Grisedale Tarn	1,768 feet	539 metres

Helvellyn

Route 74 is the most spectacular and picturesque ascent of
Helvellyn, but as detailed below it is now only accessible to
walkers. This situation has arisen because climbers coming by
car can no longer park their vehicles in Grisedale as the
landowner has blocked off the former parking pasture with a
line of large boulders. The closure of this parking area has put
considerable pressure on the limited parking available in
Patterdale and in consequence the best alternative is to leave
transport in the car park in the adjoining village of
Glenridding. This is a good starting point for the ascent of
Helvellyn and the original route can be reached in Grisedale
by way of Lanty's Tarn. But a more direct approach to
Striding Edge is by way of Mireside which leaves the village
by the lane passing the post office, when the stream on the R is
followed to the Caravan Park at Gillside. Here the cart track
on the L passes through a gate and then goes on to a white
gated cottage where it turns R and later L to a gate between
two meeting walls. Thence the path is clearly marked as it
rises across the open fell of Birkhouse Moor. On reaching
higher ground it bears L to reach the 'Hole in the Wall'
whence Route 74 is followed to Striding Edge and Helvellyn.

Map 8
Helvellyn
Routes 73 to 80

Route 73. Patterdale and Swirral Edge. Walk from Patterdale towards Glenridding and take the narrow road on L, just short of the bridge over Grisedale Beck. This skirts the grounds of Patterdale Hall, and in half a mile rises to a gate which reveals the route ahead as far as the 'Hole in the Wall' on the skyline to the west. Continue down the cart road and turn to R at the first wall, where a finger-post indicates the direction. After crossing the beck, go through the trees and ascend the slopes of the adjacent hillside to another gate. Follow the clearly marked track on L (beyond the wall) which rises across the flanks of Birkhouse Moor. When a copse appears on the skyline, climb the rather indistinct zigzags on R which join the path coming from Glenridding. Pass this copse on L and go through an iron gate which gives access to the open fell. The route is now unmistakable, and when the track bifurcates take the right branch, because it will mitigate the steepness of the final rise to the 'Hole in the Wall'. The views down into Grisedale are very fine and improve as height is gained, while the restrospect of Patterdale and the head of Ullswater is also worthy of observation from time to time. A wall runs along the top of Birkhouse Moor, and on attaining it the majestic eastern front of Helvellyn is disclosed, together with a foreshortened aspect of Striding Edge on L, and of Catchedicam and Swirral Edge on R. Go through the 'Hole in the Wall' and coast along the slopes on L until Red Tarn is seen at the foot of the Helvellyn precipices. Then bear to R over the boggy ground past its outflow and keep to the track which rises obliquely below Catchedicam to attain the ridge at the saddle. Climb the easy crags on its crest, which ultimately peters out on the vast summit plateau, and then bear to L along the edge of the precipices for the top of the mountain.

The panorama from Helvellyn is one of the most famous in Lakeland and especially notable for its combination of lake and fell. To the north the Dodds rise one after the other in an almost direct line with Blencathra, whose lateral spurs are visible at this great distance. Skiddaw stands nobly on their L, below which Bassenthwaite ripples away into the dim

Plate 144 **Routes 73** and **74** are steep. The now missing gate is known as 'the Hole in the Wall'

distance. To the south the vast plateau sinks gently beyond
the shelter and rises again to Dollywaggon Pike, on the other
side of which appear the glimmering waters of Windermere
and Esthwaite. Fairfield rises on L and is connected with St.
Sunday Crag by a high undulating ridge where Cofa Pike and
Deepdale Hause are well seen. To the east the long ridge of
High Street sweeps across the horizon, and on a clear day the
dim outline of the Pennines may be perceived above it. In the
middle distance the lower and central sections of Ullswater
are visible between Black Crag and the end of Birkhouse
Moor, while Red Tarn lies in the great hollow immediately
below. To the west, however, the vista is more arresting, for it
discloses the dominance of Scafell Pike over the galaxy of
familiar peaks clustered together in the centre of Lakeland.
Coniston Water gleams in the south-west with the bulky
Coniston Fells on its R and from which Grey Friar seems to
stand aloof. The serrated skyline then rises gradually from
Wrynose over the Crinkles and Bowfell to Scafell Pike, to fall
again to Great End, Lingmell and Glaramara before rising
sharply to the conspicuous bald top of Great Gable. Pillar is
the next clearly defined summit, followed by the High Stile
range and finally by the Grasmoor hills, where Grisedale Pike
appears as a graceful sentinel on the north-western horizon.
The foreground of this vast prospect is confused and of
comparatively little interest, Ullscarf occupying the major
position in a line with the Central Fells. Thirlmere is hidden
by the extensive western escarpments of Helvellyn, but it may
be seen by descending well to the south of the top.

Route 74. Patterdale and Striding Edge. This is one of the
most spectacular mountain walks in Lakeland and is only
dangerous under the most severe winter conditions. Follow
Route 73 as far as the 'Hole in the Wall' and then ascend the track
on L towards Striding Edge. A better variation is to keep to the
edge of the cliffs on L and to adhere to the crest of the ridge
all the way to its eastern top. Then follow its ups and downs
to the saddle, climbing down the Step above it carefully.

Catchedicam

Swirral Edge

Helvellyn

Abyss

To Gate

Plate 145 **Route 73** is stony near the top

Scramble up the eroded slopes of the Abyss, where progress is easier on the extreme L, and on emerging on the skyline turn to R past Gough's Memorial and walk up to the summit of Helvellyn. The views down on either side of Striding Edge are especially fine and justly famous for their impressiveness.

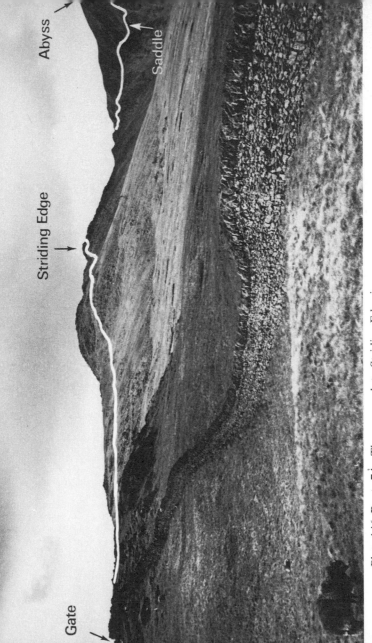

Plate 146 **Route 74**— The approach to Striding Edge is easy

Route 75. Grisedale and Dollywaggon Pike. Leave Patterdale
by Route 73 and keep straight on through the second gate,
which gives access to the deeper recesses of the dale. The route
is unmistakable, first by a cart road to Elm Howe, then as a
track to the bridge spanning the beck just beyond its junction
with the stream coming down from Ruthwaite Cove. Here the
wild prospect is magnificent with the long escarpments of
Dollywaggon Pike and Nethermost Pike descending steeply to
the west, and shut in on L by the precipitous slopes of St.
Sunday Crag, and on R by Striding Edge. Follow the tributary
to the disused shooting-box of Ruthwaite Lodge, and then
bear to L and ascend the increasingly steep and rough track. A
large cairn marks its bifurcation on the summit of the pass
just to the east of Grisedale Tarn. Take the R branch and
climb the long zigzags up to the main ridge and then leave the
path for the cairn of Dollywaggon Pike on R. Now advance
along the edge of the cliffs all the way to the summit of the
reigning peak, which is seen ahead throughout. The views to
east and west are superb and include a striking vista down
the full length of Grisedale where Place Fell rises at the head
of Ullswater far below.

Swirral Edge

Red Tarn

Nethermost Cove

Plate 147 Crossing Striding Edge by **Route 74** requires special care in the rock descent to the Saddle

Plate 148 Looking back to **Route 74** on the crest of Striding Edge

Route 76. Grasmere and Grisedale Tarn. Follow the Keswick road as far as the house on the other side of Tongue Gill and then turn in at the gate on R. A cart road leads to another gate giving access to the open fell, where a conspicuous grassy tongue is seen ahead. Keep to the well-marked track which ascends it in a direct line with Seat Sandal, and at the 1,500-feet contour bear to R along the terraced flanks of this eminence until a gap in a wall discloses Grisedale Tarn some distance below. Follow the path on its southern side and cross some boggy ground to the large cairn already mentioned in Route 75, which follow to the summit of the mountain.

Route 77. From Wythburn. There are two routes to Helvellyn from this hamlet and both of them leave the highway in the vicinity of the church. The more popular one keeps North Birkside Gill on L until the 1,250-feet contour is reached, when it bends to R below Comb Crags and thereafter sweeps round to L to join Route 75 for the summit of the mountain. Some quarter-mile short of this junction, and on L of the track, there is a spring which is alleged to be the highest in England. The other route ascends by the side of Whelpside Gill as far as its source below the summit of Helvellyn, the stream being kept on L all the way. These are the least interesting and steepest of all the ascents of this mountain.

Route 78. Thirlspot and White Side. Take the track which goes behind the inn and ascends almost due north-east. Swing round to R on approaching Fisher Gill and keep the stream on L as far as its source on the flanks of White Side. Climb the steep slopes of this subsidiary eminence until the main ridge is attained and then bear to R over Low Man for the summit of Helvellyn.

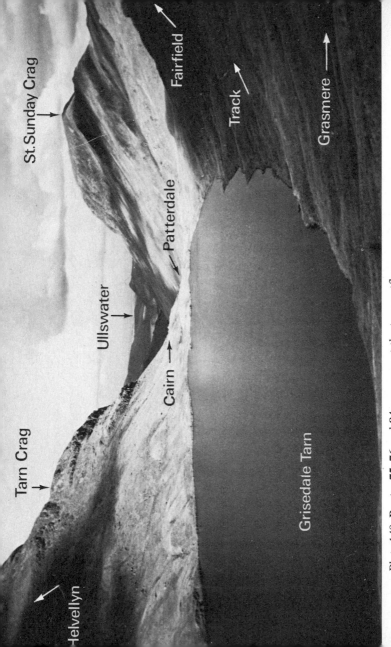

Plate 149 **Routes 75**, **76** and **84** converge at the tarn outflow

Tarn Crag

Helvellyn

St. Sunday Crag

Ullswater

Cairn →

Patterdale

Fairfield

Track

Grasmere →

Grisedale Tarn

Plate 150 **Routes 75** and **76** are well seen from Fairfield

Coniston Fells

Coniston Water

Dollywagon Pike

Track to Grisedale Tarn

Plate 151 South from **Routes 75** and **76**

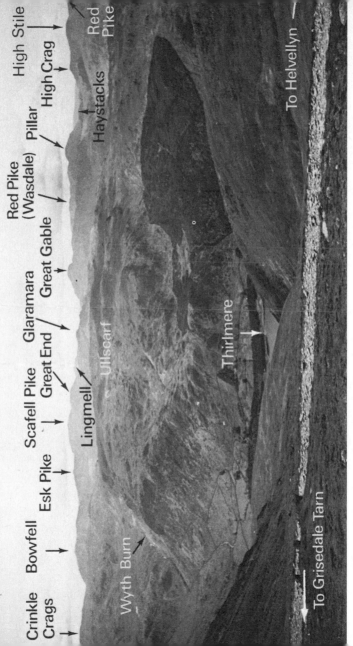

Plate 152 South-west from **Routes 75** and **76**

Plate 153   South from Helvellyn summit

Route 79. The Sticks Pass and Raise. This is the second highest pass in the Lake District and involves a long and circuitous route to Helvellyn. It would therefore be seldom chosen in preference to one of the more direct ascents and is only included for completeness. Leave the Keswick–Grasmere road at its most southerly junction with the highway going north through the Vale of St. John. Walk up the cart road to the farmstead of Stanah, and cross the gill at the end of the field behind it. Climb the zigzags as far as a sheepfold and then leave the stream on L and ascend the shoulder of Stybarrow Dodd until well above the northern tributary of Fisher Gill. On attaining the top of the pass, which is now near at hand, turn to R along the broad crest of the main ridge and walk over Raise and Low Man to reach the summit of Helvellyn.

Route 80. Glenridding and Keppel Cove. Drive up the narrow walled lane opposite the Ullswater Hotel. It is just over $1\frac{1}{2}$ miles in length and its upper section is very narrow and so rough that it requires careful driving in low gear. The car may be parked in a bay below the disused Greenside mine. Now walk up to the highest building on the R and here pick up the grassy cart track that skirts the slopes, high above the stream on the L, and ends at the sheepfold near the Dam in Keppel Cove. The ziz-zag path rising to the rim of the cove is not visible from below, but may be attained by bearing R at the cairn some distance short of the dam and opposite the riven northern slopes of Catchedicam. Thence follow the lofty skyline encircling both Keppel and Brown Coves to join Route 79 for the summit of Helvellyn.

At the time of writing the walled lane mentioned above was still in use, but it may soon be closed to all save local residents. Hence, vehicular access and parking at the mine may well be prohibited excepting to those with existing rights and any others authorised by agreement. Climbers would therefore be well advised to leave their transport in the commodious car park in Glenridding village, where Route 80 actually begins.

← Catchedicam

Plate 154 **Route 80** turns R at the cairn

Swirral Edge

Low Man

Plate 155 **Route 80** keeps to the skyline on the R. Keppel Cove Dam in the foreground

The Fairfield group

Fairfield	2,863 feet	873 metres
St. Sunday Crag	2,756 feet	840 metres
Hart Crag	2,698 feet	822 metres
Red Screes	2,541 feet	774 metres
Dove Crag	2,500 feet	762 metres
Scandale Fell	2,155 feet	657 metres
Snarker Pike	2,096 feet	639 metres
Kirkstone Pass	1,500 feet	457 metres

Fairfield

Route 81. Ambleside and Scandale Fell. Leave the town by the Kirkstone road and turn to L on approaching the old church. Take the left branch at the fork, which in half a mile leads to the farmstead of Nook End, and on the other side of it cross Scandale Beck by Low Sweden Bridge. Thereafter follow the track northwards with Low Pike ahead as the first eminence to be scaled. As height is gained there are beautiful views of the Rothay Valley and Rydal on L, while low down on R the track for Patterdale is seen rising to the Scandale Pass. The retrospect of Windermere also is delightful with its surface rippling away into the dim distance in the south. Keep to the crest of the ridge for Scandale Fell and note the two rocky knobs of Little Hart Crag above the pass on R. Continue ahead until the cairn on the broad main ridge is attained and then bear to L above Dove Crag and Hart Crag, which disclose splendid prospects to R; first down Dovedale to Brothers Water, and then down Deepdale to Patterdale backed by Place Fell. Bear to L again after traversing Hart Crag and observe the fine precipitous bastion of Greenhow End dropping down on R. Then make for the flat top of Fairfield,

Scandale Fell

Little Hart Crag

Snarker Pike

Windermere

Plate 156 **Route 81** as seen from Windermere.

Map 9
Fairfield
Routes 81 to 89

which is crowned by four cairns that can be very confusing in mist.

The panorama from Fairfield to east and west is not dissimilar to that from Helvellyn, but this mountain blocks much of the northern prospect and at the same time admirably reveals the topography of its grand subsidiary ridges. The view from the edge of the precipices enclosing the combe on the east is striking and will be a surprise to newcomers. It discloses the best aspect of Cofa Pike on L, beyond which the ground falls steeply to Deepdale Hause, to rise again gracefully to the summit of St. Sunday Crag. The vista to the south is disappointing because the long escarpment of Great Rigg cuts out all the valleys immediately below it. The distant view of Windermere, Esthwaite and Coniston Water is, however, a delight and especially on a clear day when the sunlight is reflected by them no less than by the great expanse of Morecambe Bay in the background.

Route 82. Rydal and Nab Scar. Leave the village by ascending the steep road between the church and Rydal Mount on L and Rydall Hall on R. Pass through a gate, turn to L through another, and then climb the steep path between two walls which leads to a stile giving access to the open fell. Continue the ascent until Nab Scar is attained, and there linger to rest and admire the magnificent prospect to the south. The most striking features are Rydal Water and Grasmere over 1,000 feet below, together with the superlative vista down the Rothay Valley to Windermere. Heron Pike rising to the north is the next objective, and its ascent still further widens the extensive retrospect, which now includes Alcock Tarn below on R. Thereafter the route is unmistakable, first along the crest of the ridge to Great Rigg and eventually to the summit of Fairfield.

Route 83. Grasmere and Stone Arthur. Take the road beside the Swan Hotel and in a short distance turn to R between some beautifully situated houses. Follow the north bank of

Greenhead Gill for half a mile and then climb the steep slopes of Stone Arthur on L. On reaching its top, keep to the crest of the ridge for Great Rigg and then follow Route 82 for the summit of Fairfield.

Route 84. Grasmere and Grisedale Tarn. Follow Route 76 until the tarn is revealed below and then climb the rough slopes on R beside a stone wall which leads to the summit of the mountain.

Route 85. Patterdale and St. Sunday Crag. Follow Route 73 for a short distance and turn in at a gate on L where an iron fence runs across the field. Go through a gate in this fence and pick up the rather indistinct track which rises beneath some scanty trees and eventually reaches a stile in a wall on the brow of Thornhow End. Skirt the northern face of these crags by walking along a wide terrace which peters out near the top of this eminence. Then advance over the broad grassy crest of the ridge towards St. Sunday Crag, which rises to the south-west, keeping to the edge of the slopes high above Grisedale. The views to R of the precipitous eastern cliffs of the Helvellyn range are superb, while those on L of the craggy combes below Route 81 are also very fine. The most delectable vista from the summit of this mountain is, however, in retrospect since it reveals the head of Ullswater far below together with its graceful bends in the background. The ridge narrows in the descent to Deepdale Hause and discloses a grand prospect of the wild combe at the head of Deepdale already referred to in Route 81. Cofa Pike rises ahead as a sharp point on the Fairfield ridge; climb the stony slopes and traverse it to set foot on the summit of the reigning peak, noting the bird's-eye view of Grisedale Tarn far below on R.

St.Sunday Crag

Grisedale

Thornhow End

Patterdale

Ullswater

Plate 157 **Route 85** opens up varied views of Helvellyn

Great Mell Fell

Gowbarrow Fell

Little Mell Fell

Birk Fell

Place Fell

Thornhow End

To St. Sunday Crag

Ullswater

Griesedale

Plate 158 **Route 85**—an excellent viewpoint

Plate 159 **Route 85** faces the descent to Grisedale Tarn

Plate 160 **Route 85**—Cofa Pike

Route 86. Patterdale and Deepdale. Leave the village by the Kirkstone road and diverge to R along a cart road about half a mile to the south. This threads the lower reaches of the wide green strath of Deepdale and passes some cottages on R before terminating at Wall End. Continue along the grassy track on the north side of the stream with Greenhow End rising ahead and with fine views into the great high combe on R. On approaching this rocky bastion, cross the main stream and follow its southern tributary which has its source in Link Cove below Hart Crag. Climb the steep slopes near a gully on L and turn the southern extremity of this crag. Then scramble along the edge of its cliffs on R to join Route 81 for the summit of Fairfield.

Route 87. Patterdale and Dovedale. Leave the village by the Kirkstone road, and on approaching Brothers Water desert the highway and take the cart road on R which passes beneath the trees fringing the shore of the lake. Go as far as the first barn beyond Hartsop Hall and then bear R up the grassy cart track to some quarry workings. Now enter the woods and keep to the wall on the L until you reach a gate in a cross wall, whence follow the well-marked path that swings round to the R across the steep slopes of Hartsop above How. Keep the beck on the L until you enter the boulder-strewn Hunsett Cove, with Dove Crag towering overhead. On reaching it bear R and scramble up the rough slopes of the combe, and on attaining the crest of the ridge pick up Route 81 for Fairfield. A more romantic approach follows the cart track to its terminus in a secluded Campers' Dell. Thence it continues as a sketchy path on the north side of the beck, rises steeply through the trees round the base of the Stangs and joins the former route below Dove Crag.

Hart Crag · Link Cove · Scrubby Crag · Greenhow End · Fairfield · Cofa Pike · Deepdale Hause

Plate 161 **Route 86**—The head of Deepdale

Dove Crag   Hart Crag

The Stangs

Hartsop Hall

Plate 162 **Route 87** — Dovedale. The crag has many rock climbs

An attractive alternative to Routes 86 and 87 is the easy traverse of Hartsop above How, an undulating grassy ridge separating the two dales. It has the merit of disclosing a bird's eye view of each, together with Y Gully on Dove Crag on the L, and Link Cove on the R. The latter is one of the wildest in this part of Lakeland and enclosed by the shattered front of Hart Crag, the cliffs of Scrubby Crag and the terminal precipices of Greenhow End.

Route 88. Brothers Water, Caiston Glen and the Scandale Pass. Proceed along the Kirkstone road until a stile is reached on R about half a mile beyond the inn. Cross the fields to a bridge spanning Kirkstone Beck, and climb up beside the stream coming down Caiston Glen. Follow this almost to its source, taking whichever bank is more convenient. On attaining the Scandale Pass on the skyline, cross the stile on R and follow the high wall past the small tarn at the foot of Little Hart Crag. Breast the slopes ahead as far as the cairn above Dove Crag and there join Route 81 for Fairfield.

Route 89. The Kirkstone Pass and Red Screes. This craggy hill rises to the north-west of the Kirkstone Pass Inn, and although there is no track ascending its steep flanks a good climber will have no difficulty in finding a way to the summit. This commands a superlative full-length prospect of Windermere, a part only of its upper reaches being hidden by the ridge of Wansfell. In addition to the bird's-eye view of the Kirkstone Pass far below, it reveals much of the eastern and western panoramas as seen from Helvellyn. The descent for Fairfield is to the north-west, where a wall may be picked up which falls to the Scandale Pass. Here Route 88 is joined and traversed to the reigning peak.

High Hartsop Dodd

Scandale Pass

Red Screes

Kirkstone Pass

Caiston Glen

Brothers Water

Plate 163 **Route 88** is on the R of the road to Kirkstone Pass

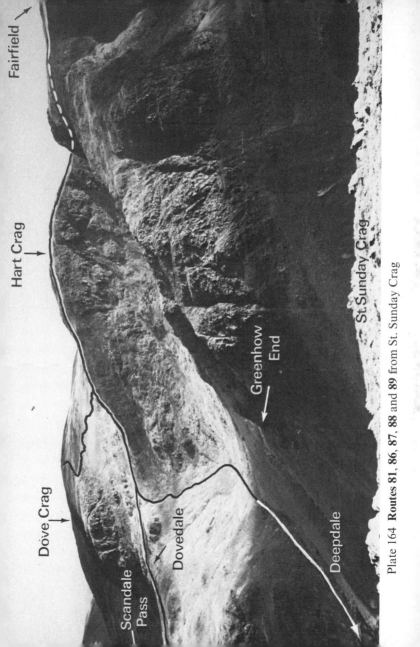

Plate 164 **Routes 81, 86, 87, 88** and **89** from St. Sunday Crag

High Street (North)

High Street	2,719 feet	829 metres
High Raise	2,634 feet	803 metres
Kidsty Pike	2,560 feet	780 metres
Mardale Ill Bell	2,496 feet	761 metres
Weather Hill	2,174 feet	663 metres
Nan Bield Pass	2,100 feet	640 metres

High Street (North)

Route 90. Patterdale and Pasture Beck. Leave the village by the Kirkstone road and at the second fork before Brothers Water take the left branch for Low Hartsop. Pass through the hamlet and park your car in a large space beyond the last cottage. Pass through a gate and bear to R along a cart road which eventually crosses Pasture Beck. Keep the stream on L and follow the track which swings round to R in a short distance and rises to a gate. This gives access to the wild stretches of the valley between Gray Crag on L and Low Hartsop Dodd on R, where Raven Crag is a conspicuous outcrop of rock high above the stream. Keep this on R and follow the sketchy track which threads Threshthwaite Cove and rises to the dip in the skyline ahead. Bear to L here and scale the loose shaly slopes of Thornthwaite Crag, which is crowned by a high slender cairn. This view-point is a revelation to the newcomer, for it opens up an extensive panorama to the south where Windermere glitters away into the dim distance backed by Morecambe Bay, and also discloses much of the topography of the High Street range to the north-east. Now drop down and advance across the boggy ground in this direction, picking up the stone wall which runs up to the summit of the mountain.

The panorama from High Street is interesting, but owing to

Raven Crag

Thornthwaite Crag

Thresthwaite Cove

Plate 165 **Route 90** follows Pasture Beck to the gaps in the skyline

Map 10
High Street (North)
Routes 90 to 97

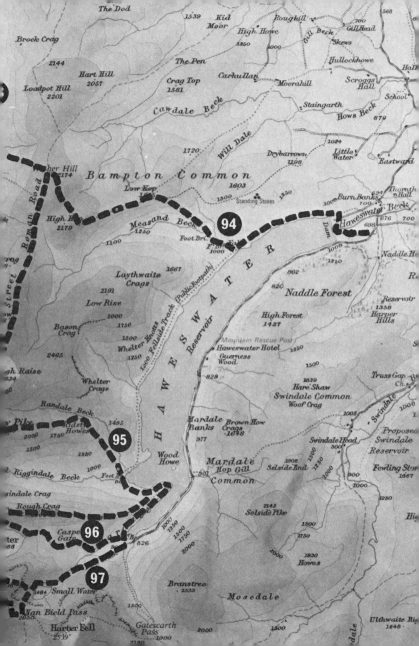

the width of the plateau it is desirable to walk some distance
from the cairn to see all but the western section of the arc. To
the north the high ridge undulates as far as the eye can see
with the conspicuous stone wall running along its many ups
and downs and where traces of the Roman road may be
perceived immediately on its left. Place Fell, the Knott and
Kidsty Pike are prominent in the foreground, while
Saddleback, Carrock Fell and Great Mell Fell rise on the
distant horizon. To the south the view is largely obscured by
Mardale Ill Bell and Harter Fell, Froswick and Ill Bell and the
ridge running up to Thornythwaite Crag, but the lower
reaches of Windermere are visible. To the east Rough Crag
drops steeply to the Saddle and its further hummocks rise
above the head of Haweswater, a glimpse of which is seen on
L. The background is rather confused by the wild moorland
stretches of the Shap Fells, above which the Pennine skyline
discloses Cross Fell on L and Ingleborough on R. The
extensive prospect to the west is, however, more fascinating
because it comprises the full length of the Fairfield and
Helvellyn groups, dominated by the Central Fells. Taken as a
whole, the most outstanding features are as follows from left
to right. The Coniston Fells are prominent on L of Red Screes
whose summit is seen beyond the stone-walled top of Caudale
Moor. The Crinkles, Bowfell and the Scafells then rise above
the dip of the Scandale Pass with the bald top of Great Gable
between Dove Crag and Hart Crag. Then comes the scarped
front of Fairfield with a glimpse of High Stile and Red Pike
on R above the Grisedale Pass. Thereafter the Helvellyn range
sweeps across the horizon where Great Dodd is backed by the
massive form of Skiddaw in the north-west.

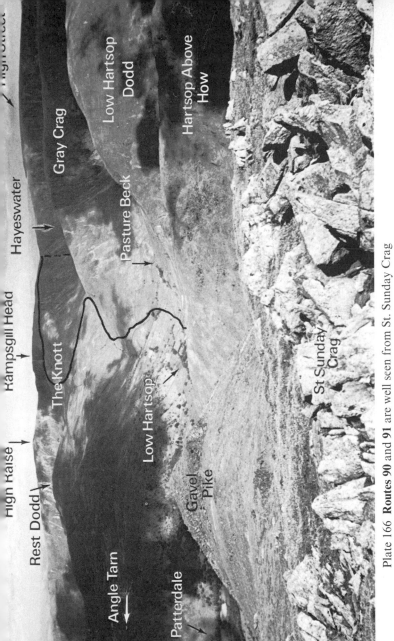

High Street

Rampsgill Head

Hayeswater

Gray Crag

Low Hartsop Dodd

Pasture Beck

Hartsop Above How

High Raise

Rest Dodd

The Knott

Low Hartsop

St Sunday Crag

Angle Tarn

Patterdale

Gavel Pike

Plate 166 **Routes 90** and **91** are well seen from St. Sunday Crag

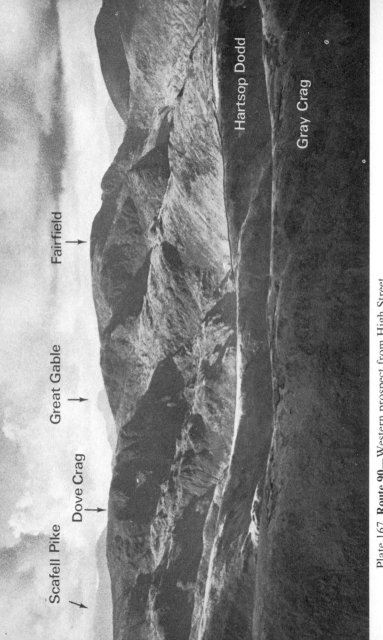

Scafell Pike   Dove Crag   Great Gable   Fairfield   Hartsop Dodd   Gray Crag

Plate 167 **Route 90**— Western prospect from High Street

Route 91. Patterdale and Hayes Water. Follow Route 90 as
far as the hamlet of Low Hartsop. Now keep to the cart road
on L which passes through a gate, and beyond a Water Board
building crosses the tributary stream coming down from
Hayes Water. The track rises to R and ends at the dam. Two
routes are now open to the climber, who may skirt the
northern banks of the tarn and then scramble straight up the
shattered face of the ridge to the east, emerging on the skyline
near the stone wall which is followed to R for the summit of
High Street, or he may prefer the less strenuous course of
climbing to L towards the Knott, passing round it to L and so
gaining the track by the same wall which runs up to the
reigning peak.

Route 92. Patterdale and Angle Tarn. This is the most direct
and popular route to High Street. Turn to L along the road
which diverges from the highway in the village, and at
Rooking ascend either of the two paths on R. These rise to
Boardale Hause, which discloses a fine retrospect of the head
of Ullswater. After traversing a number of craggy hummocks,
pass round the Pikes on L, when Angle Tarn soon appears in
a grassy hollow below. Bear to L and skirt its northern shore,
passing Buck Crag and Satura Crag for the Knott straight
ahead. Hereabouts there are some fine vistas down the wide
green strath of Bannerdale, and many walkers may choose to
diverge to L to climb Rest Dodd, which reveals an even better
prospect of the two dales to the north. Then join Route 91 and
climb up to a gate on the brow of the Knott where the track
swings round behind it for High Street.

There is an alternative approach for those coming from the
south. Park your car beside the telephone kiosk near Brothers
Water and walk back to Hartsop. After passing the first
cottage on the L, turn L up the cart track. In about a mile take
the R fork which is grassy and rises gently to Boardale Hause.

Plate 168 Helvellyn from the Straits of Riggindale—**Routes 92, 93, 94 and 95**

Plate 169 **Route 92** — Helvellyn from Angle Tarn — a popular resting place for fell walkers

Route 93. Howtown and Weather Hill. Pass through a gate near the Howtown Hotel which gives access to Fusedale due south. Follow the track with the beck first on L and then on R. In a mile and a half a tributary comes down on L and keep to it for a short distance. Then cross the stream and climb straight up the fellside for Weather Hill. The view to R into the deep recesses of Rampsgill Head is very fine, with the conspicuous spur known as the Nab on R. On attaining the ridge, turn to R along its crest and follow the Roman road over High Raise and Kidsty Pike, diverging to L here for the cairn, which reveals perhaps the most comprehensive aspect of High Street. Then skirt the head of Riggindale and drop down to the narrow col to pick up Route 92 for the summit.

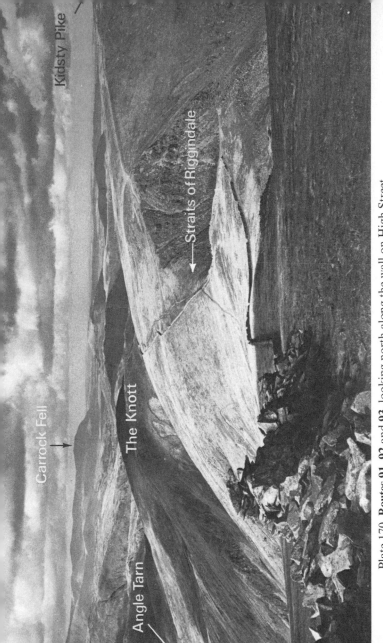

Plate 170 **Routes 91**, **92** and **93**, looking north along the wall on High Street

Route 94. Mardale and Measand Beck. Leave the Haweswater
Hotel and walk along the Penrith road as far as the new dam,
and at the first convenient place descend to the valley to cross
the small bridge at its foot. Walk up the northern slopes to
gain the new track and turn to L above the lake. Measand
Beck is about a mile along this track, cross it and ascend the
south bank, recrossing it again by a footbridge. Then climb
obliquely over the grassy slopes to Low Kop and keep to the
high ground westwards for Weather Hill. Here join Route 93
for High Street.

Bampton Common

Measand Beck

Haweswater

Plate 171 **Route 94** begins at the dam

Route 95. Mardale and Kidsty Pike. Leave the Haweswater Hotel and walk southwards along the road to its terminus. Pass through a gate and turn to R along a wall, crossing the beck by a new footbridge. Turn to R again and keep to the track which passes above and behind the wooded spur jutting out into the lake. Drop down to the footbridge over Riggindale Beck, and keeping Randale Beck on R climb the grassy slopes of Kidsty Howes. On attaining the high ground, bear to L high above this stream until Kidsty Pike appears ahead. Here join Route 93 for the summit of the reigning peak.

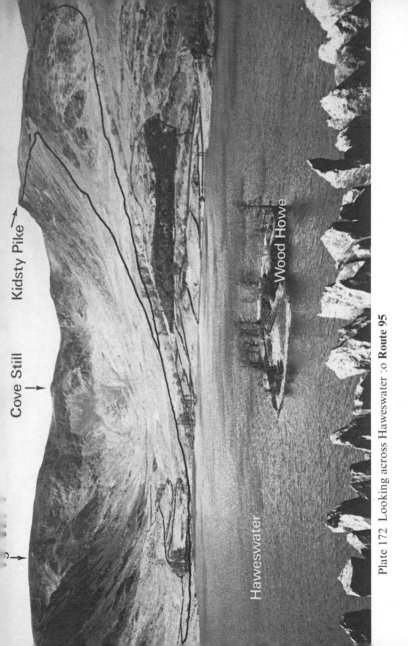

Cove Still →   Kidsty Pike →

Wood Howe

Haweswater

Plate 172   Looking across Haweswater to **Route 95**

Route 96. Mardale and Rough Crag. Follow Route 95 to the
footbridge at the head of Haweswater, and after crossing it
turn to L. Keep to the stream for half a mile and then follow
its tributary over the grassy ground of Caspel Gate until Blea
Water appears ahead. Then diverge to R for the Saddle and
afterwards climb the craggy escarpment which rises to the
skyline immediately to the east of the summit of High Street.
Those wishing to traverse the full length of Rough Crag
should follow Route 95 to the wooded spur and then climb up
to its crest by the wall on L.

Route 97. Mardale and Nan Bield. Follow Route 95 to the end
of the road, and after passing through the gate keep to the
track which rises to the south-west as far as Small Water with
Harter Fell on L and the stream on R nearly all the way. Skirt
the north-western shore of the tarn and climb the zigzags to
Nan Bield, which is the prominent dip in the skyline. Then
turn sharp to R up the craggy declivities of Mardale Ill Bell,
which discloses a fine view of the Ill Bell Range, with
Kentmere and its reservoir down on L. Traverse the broad
top, keeping well to R above Blea Water, and then follow the
wall on the skyline which leads to the summit of High Street.
A short cut may be taken from Small Water up the rocky spur
of Mardale Ill Bell, but this variation misses the vista of
Kentmere.

Plate 173 **Route 97** — Retrospect of Small Water from the track below Nan Bield

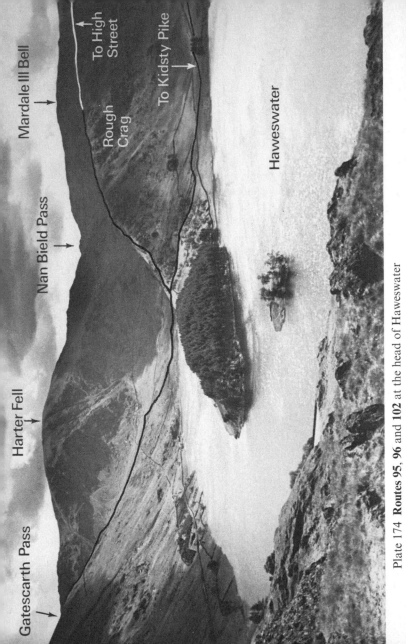

Gatescarth Pass

Harter Fell

Nan Bield Pass

Mardale Ill Bell

Rough Crag

To High Street

To Kidsty Pike

Haweswater

Plate 174 **Routes 95**, **96** and **102** at the head of Haweswater

Plate 175 **Route 96** keeps to the crest of Rough Crag and the Saddle

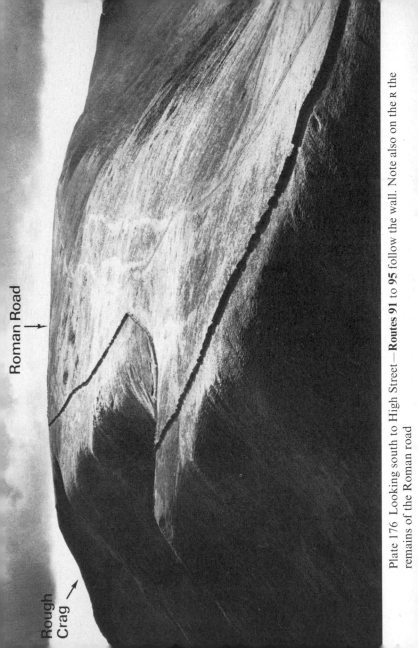

Rough Crag →

Roman Road ←

Plate 176 Looking south to High Street—**Routes 91** to **95** follow the wall. Note also on the R the remains of the Roman road

Plate 177 **Routes 95, 96, 97, 101, and 102** all start at the Road Terminus

High Street (South) and Harter Fell

High Street	2,719 feet	829 metres
Thornthwaite Beacon	2,569 feet	783 metres
Mardale Ill Bell	2,496 feet	761 metres
Ill Bell	2,476 feet	755 metres
Froswick	2,359 feet	719 metres
Yoke	2,309 feet	704 metres
Harter Fell	2,539 feet	774 metres

High Street (South)

Route 98. Kentmere and Nan Bield. Leave the village with the church and the River Kent on L. Cross a bridge and when the road surface bifurcates take the L branch (the R branch goes to Long Sleddale). In a short distance cross the fields on L to view some pretty falls, and on regaining the road proceed northwards to Overend, the last farm in the dale. Here the road forks again, but take the R branch this time and after another mile avoid the quarry road on R. Traverse the western flanks of Harter Fell with the Kentmere Reservoir low down on the left and continue northwards to Nan Bield, where turn to L and pick up Route 97 for High Street.

Route 99. Troutbeck and Ill Bell. Leave the village at Town Head and cross the Kirkstone road. Avoid the first turn on L which goes to Troutbeck Park, but bear to L after crossing the bridge over Trout Beck and join another road at Long Green Head. Advance northwards for nearly a mile; then turn off to R and scale Lowther Brow as a prelude to the higher slopes of Yoke. Keep to the crest of the ridge for Ill Bell, whose summit is characterised by three cairns. The retrospect is splendid and discloses much the same view of Windermere as Thornthwaite

← Ill Bell

Yoke →

Rainsbarrow Crag →

Nan Bield Pass

Kentmere Reservoir

To Kentmere ↓

Plate 178 **Route 98**—The reservoir seldom overflows

Map 11
High Street (South)
Routes 98 to 103

Crag. Continue northwards but pass to the right of this top and beyond it pick up Route 90 for High Street.

A variation that saves height is preferable for climbers coming from Windermere by car. Drive along the Kendal road and take the first turn on the L. At the subsequent fork bear R past the reservoir and go on for another mile. Turn your car in the wide gate on the L and park it on the nearby grassy verge. Now walk up the walled cart track that rises to Garburn, and on reaching the cairn on the L, just short of its crest, ascend the grassy path which later drops down to a beck and beyond it rises to a large cairn. Here take the R branch over the grassy hummocks until you reach a stone wall. Keep to the L of it as far as the point where it bears sharp L. Cross the high stile and pick up the path on the other side which rises gently to Yoke and thence to Ill Bell. If you wish to save height, bear L on the track that contours round Yoke and regains the main path at the col overlooking Kentmere Reservoir. On attaining Ill Bell, traverse Froswick on Route 99 as indicated above.

Route 100. Troutbeck and Thornthwaite Crag. Follow Route 99 to the foot of Lowther Brow and then keep straight on up the valley with Troutbeck Tongue and Hagg Gill on L. Cross this stream by a footbridge about a mile farther on and keep it on R for another mile and a half. Then commence the steep ascent of the Roman road which traverses the western flanks of Froswick. Climb up to Thornthwaite Crag, which towers ahead, and join Route 90 for High Street.

Routes 99 and 100 are known locally as 'Bootleggers Walk'.

High Street

Froswick

Thornthwaite Beacon

Plate 179 **Route 99** from Ill Bell

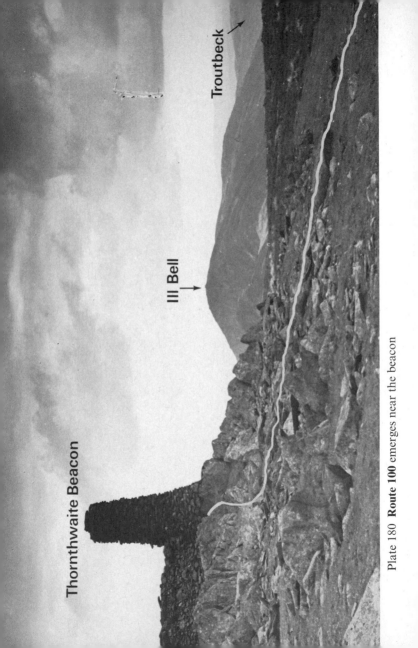

Thornthwaite Beacon

Ill Bell

Troutbeck

Plate 180 **Route 100** emerges near the beacon

Harter Fell—Mardale

Route 101. From Nan Bield. Climb the track rising to the south-east from the top of the Pass and keep the crags on the R all the way to the first prominent cairn. Thence walk up the rising grassy plateau to the summit cairn which is built of the iron fence that formerly enclosed the grazing ground on the R and has now been replaced by a wire fence. Harter Fell is notable for two prospects: the one of Mardale immediately below to the north with the long reaches of Haweswater glittering away into the distance, and flanked on the west by High Street at its best, and on the east by the featureless slopes about Guerness Wood; the other from its southern tip called the Knowe, which reveals the dalehead of Kentmere to advantage together with its shapely enclosing peaks on the west.

Route 102. Mardale and Gate Scarth Pass. Follow Route 95 to the end of the road, and after passing through the gate take the grass-covered cart track on L which winds upwards between Branstree on L and Harter Fell on R. On reaching the cairn on the top of the pass, turn sharp to R and follow the wire fence to Adam Seat. Here you turn R and keep to the path beside the fence which takes a straight line all the way to the summit of Harter Fell.

Route 103. Long Sleddale and Gate Scarth. Leave Sadgill, the last farm in the dale, by the old grass-covered quarry road which winds up the valley between two prominent stone walls. Goat Scar and Raven Crag are the two rocky outcrops high up on L, while the shattered cliffs of Buckbarrow frown down on R. The River Sprint provides plenty of water music until the disused quarry workings are reached. Avoid the track on R and leave the quarries on L, but ascend the zigzags over the grassy brow of the hill ahead and traverse some boggy ground before the cairn on Gate Scarth is attained. Then bear to L and follow Route 102 for Harter Fell.

Plate 181 **Route 101**—Haweswater from Harter Fell

Plate 182 **Route 101** — High Street and Blea Water from Harter Fell

Plate 183 **Route 102**—Track to Harter Fell keeps to the fence from Adam Seat

← Goat Scar

Tarn Crag →

Buckbarrow →

Raven Crag →

To Gate Scarth Pass

Road giving acess to Gate Scarth Pass →

Sadgill

Plate 184 **Route 103** begins at Sadgill where the tarmac road ends

The Langdale Pikes

High White Stones	2,500 feet	762 metres
Harrison Stickle	2,401 feet	732 metres
Ullscarf	2,370 feet	722 metres
Pike o' Stickle	2,323 feet	708 metres
Pavey Ark	2,288 feet	697 metres
Greenup	2,000 feet	610 metres
Stake Pass	1,576 feet	480 metres
Stickle Tarn	1,540 feet	469 metres
Silver How	1,300 feet	396 metres

The Langdale Pikes

Route 104. by Mill Gill. Leave the road in Great Langdale and walk up the drive to the New Dungeon Ghyll Hotel. Pass to the R of the white cottage and follow the new path beside the stream which later joins the old track near the waterfalls.Thereafter traverse some boggy ground and climb the clearly defined path which sweeps round to R to join the beck again where it emerges from Stickle Tarn. This is a singularly wild viewpoint and reveals the great gullied cliffs of Pavey Ark on the other side of the tarn where it is connected with Harrison Stickle by a high ridge. Turn to L and walk due west over the grassy slopes at the base of the reigning peak, but skirt its crags on R and climb the scree beside them to attain its horizontal summit.

The fine profile of these hills and their relationship to the adjacent Crinkle-Bowfell Group is well seen from the shores of Windermere in the vicinity of Low Wood. On entering the valley of Great Langdale beyond Chapel Stile, their majestic proportions are still more impressive and reveal at a glance the two principal routes to the summit. It will therefore perhaps surprise the newcomer to find that the panorama

Crinkle Crags

Pike O'Blisco

Lingmoor

Bowfell

Great
End

Esk Pike

Allen
Crags

Pike O'Stickle

Harrison
Stickle

Pavey
Ark

Windermere

Plate 185 The western panorama from Windermere

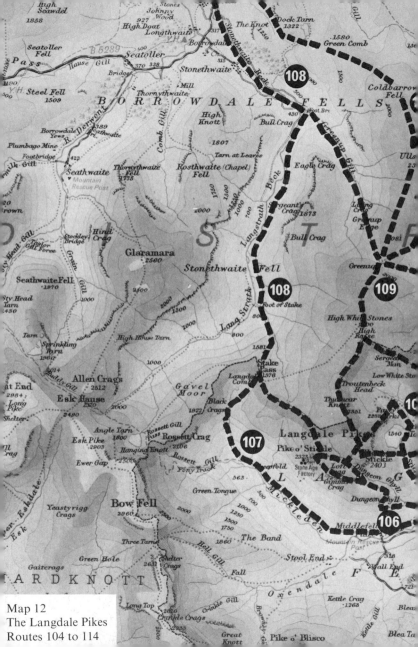

Map 12
The Langdale Pikes
Routes 104 to 114

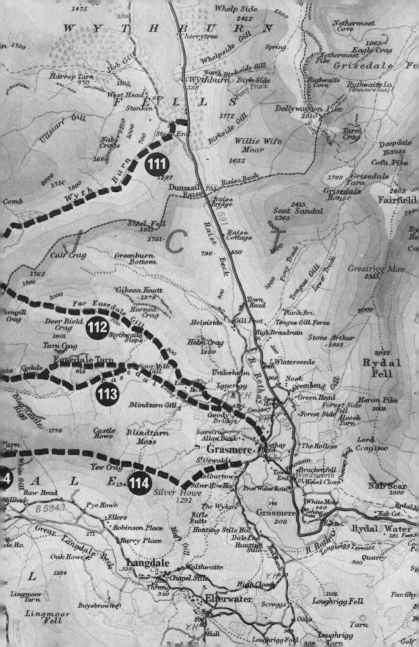

from Harrison Stickle is one of the most restricted in Lakeland and completely belies its splendour from the east. This is due mainly to its inferior height when compared with the engirdling hills, and to the extensive lofty plateau which obscures the valleys in all directions, save to the south-east where the ground falls away to unfold the finest vista from the peak itself. This comprises the wide green patterned strath of Great Langdale which leads the eye first to Elterwater and Windermere, then to R to Esthwaite and finally to the luminous surface of Blea Tarn, low down on the R. The western prospect from Bow Fell to the Gables is the best of the distant views, and its skyline also discloses Scafell Pike above Ewer Gap, Great End above Esk Hause and the Gables above the long ridge rising to Glaramara.

Note—The lower section of this route has eroded so badly owing to its tremendous usage that is has been closed for the time being. But a new path has been made which joins the original one in its higher reaches. However, even this section may be avoided by ascending Route 106 to the Ghyll whence turn R and follow the wall until the old path is encountered.

Route 105. by Pavey Ark. Follow Route 104 to Stickle Tarn where the topography of Pavey Ark reveals a prominent ledge known as Jacks Rake rising from R to L across its precipitous face, together with a great rift in the crags on R known as the Scree Gully. The ascent of the latter forms a sporting variation to the previous route, and while it is free from danger it has the advantage of a close view of the crags which are popular with the rock-climbing fraternity. Skirt the shore of the tarn and ascend the bewildering array of boulders to the mouth of the gully. Keep to L while scaling the floor of the chasm as far as the gigantic boulders blocking its exit. Then go over to R corner and scramble over them to attain the track, which bears to L above the Ark, and rises to the south in a direct line with the summit of Harrison Stickle.

Note—Erosion has made the ascent of Jacks Rake too dangerous for fell walkers and should be avoided.

Pavey Ark

Harrison Stickle

Loft Crag

Gimmer

Mill Gill

Dungeon Ghyll

New Hotel

Great Langdale

Plate 186 **Routes 104** and **105** seen from Chapel Stile

Plate 187 **Route 104** begins at the New Dungeon Ghyll Hotel

Plate 188   **Route 104**—The new track follows the stream on the ʀ, but its erosion is already considerable

Pavey Ark

Scree Gully

Jacks Rake

Stickle Tarn

Plate 189 **Route 105**—Goes over Pavey Ark from Stickle Tarn

Plate 190 **Route 104** passes Stickle Tarn on ʀ

Cold Pike

Great Knott

Long Top

Harrison Stickle

Stickle Tarn

To Mill Gill

Route 106. by Dungeon Ghyll. Leave the New Hotel by Route 104, but keep straight ahead across the fields until the path crosses the ghyll. Then climb with it on R, past the almost hidden waterfall, but desert it higher up to follow the path which diverges to L and swings round again to reach the col immediately on R of Loft Crag. Now leave the track and walk to L on to its top which dominates Gimmer Crag; then keep to the edge of the cliffs and afterwards ascend Pike o' Stickle. The view to the south-east is much finer than that from Harrison Stickle because it discloses the grand western façade of Gimmer which frowns upon the walled strath of the dale some 2,000 feet below. It also reveals a bird's-eye view of Mickleden to the west which terminates with the fine rift of Rossett Gill. Descend in an easterly direction for Harrison Stickle, cross the stream and the intervening boggy ground, and then climb up to the twin cairns on its flat summit ridge.

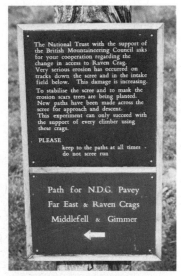

Plate 191 Erosion warning

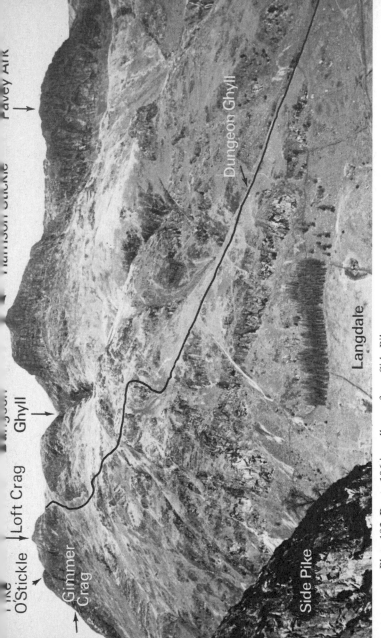

Pike O'Stickle | Loft Crag | Gimmer Crag | Pavey Ark | Harrison Stickle | Dungeon Ghyll | Dungeon Ghyll | Langdale | Side Pike

Plate 192 **Route 106** is well seen from Side Pike

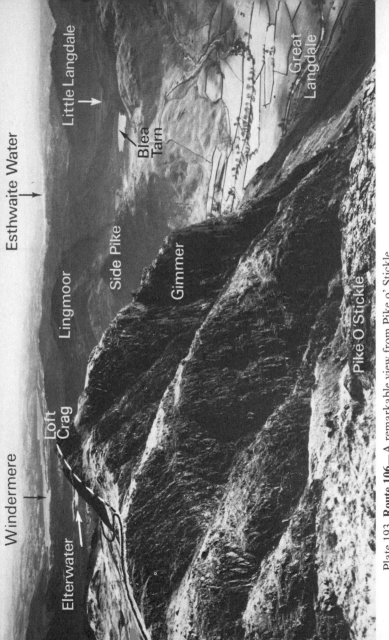

Windermere

Esthwaite Water

Little Langdale

Great Langdale

Blea Tarn

Loft Crag

Lingmoor

Side Pike

Elterwater

Gimmer

Pike O' Stickle

Plate 193 **Route 106**—A remarkable view from Pike o' Stickle

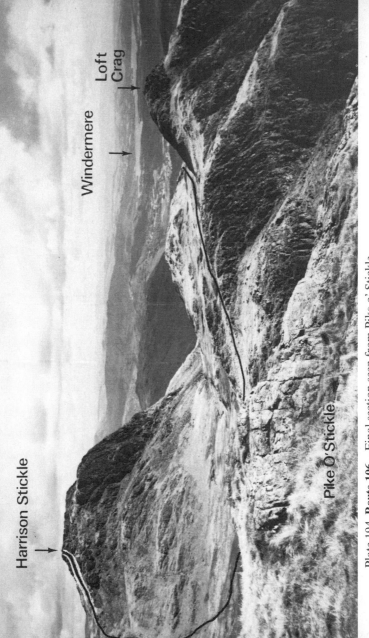

Harrison Stickle

Windermere

Loft Crag

Pike O' Stickle

Plate 194 **Route 106**—Final section seen from Pike o' Stickle

Route 107. Mickleden and the Stake Pass. Take the track on L
of the Old Dungeon Ghyll Hotel which runs behind a stone
wall for half the length of Mickleden. Continue ahead over
the green strath as far as a sheepfold situated at the end of the
valley where the track forks, the left branch rising in the bed
of Rossett Gill, and the right one zigzagging up the fellside to
Langdale Combe and the Stake. Climb the latter beside the
stream, and on reaching the cairn marking the summit of the
pass turn sharp to R and take a direct line for Pike o' Stickle
to join Route 106 for the reigning peak. The views down on R
into Mickleden are very fine during the latter part of the
ascent.

Route 108. Rosthwaite and the Stake Pass. Follow Route 31 as
far as the bridge at the foot of the Stake. Ascend the winding
path which rises to the cairn mentioned in Route 107, and
follow it to Harrison Stickle. During the walk up Langstrath
note the delightful Olympian Pool which provides excellent
bathing in hot weather.

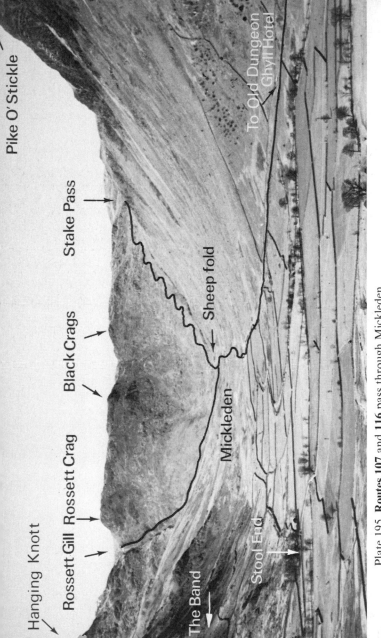

Pike O'Stickle

Hanging Knott

Rossett Gill Rossett Crag

Black Crags

Stake Pass

Sheep fold

Mickleden

To Old Dungeon Ghyll Hotel

Stool End

The Band

Plate 195 **Routes 107** and **116** pass through Mickleden

Route 109. Greenup and High White Stones. Leave Rosthwaite
by the bridge to Hazel Bank, and after crossing it turn to R
and follow the track by Stonethwaite Beck. In a mile and a
half pass the new bridge on R over Greenup Gill and climb the
track ahead for the Lining Crag. On approaching this rocky
bastion, bear to L and scale the steep slopes beside a runnel
which comes down on its left. As height is gained note the
large number of moraine heaps down on the right at the head
of the combe, and on attaining the easier slopes above keep to
the south over some marshy ground for the guide-post on
Greenup. Then turn sharp to R up the slopes of the hill and
follow a wire fence, which on bending away to L discloses the
cairn on High White Stones straight ahead. Walk up to this
fine belvedere and pause for a moment to view the
comprehensive panorama, for it might well be the Lakeland
axis since it is high enough to overlook all the nearer
eminences, including the Langdale Pikes to the south, and
reveals a great number of the familiar peaks engirdling the
whole horizon. The Central Fells and their satellites appear to
the west and north-west, the two massive sentinels of Skiddaw
and Saddleback rise on the northern skyline, while the whole
of the Helvellyn and Fairfield ranges close the prospect to the
east. Proceed due south over the vast undulating moorland
solitudes and leave Pavey Ark on L to attain the summit of
Harrison Stickle.

Note—The moorland dominated by High White Stones is
known as High Raise.

Route 110. Dock Tarn and Ullscarf. Climb the steep track by
the stream which comes down the hillside on R of Hazel Bank
in Rosthwaite. Go through a gap in the wall on the skyline and
turn to R to pass a sheepfold some distance along this
wall. Leave the beck and ascend obliquely to L across the
grassy hummocks to a stile over a wall below some beetling
crags. Follow a clearly marked path on the other side and
skirt the eminence on L; then cross a small col and descend

slightly on the edge of some marshy ground until Dock Tarn appears through a narrow gap ahead. Pick up a track to R of it and cross the stream at the outflow. Climb the hummocks on the far side and then traverse the rough slopes rising to Green Comb. Now continue the ascent in a south-easterly direction for Coldbarrow Fell, and keeping to the high ground walk over Ullscarf and finally drop down to the guide-post on Greenup, thereafter following Route 109 for the Langdale Pikes. The retrospect of the head of Borrowdale during the first part of the ascent is exceptionally fine and reveals the dominance of Great Gable, while the vista along Langstrath from a point near the outflow of Dock Tarn is magnificent and one of the many surprises of this interesting route.

Route 111. Wythburn and Greenup. This ascent is unmistakable and follows the stream coming down the wide valley to the south-west of the head of Thirlmere. Leave the road skirting its western shore near its southern junction with the main Keswick–Grasmere highway. Follow the cart road to the farm of Steel End and then bear to R to pick up the stream. Keep it on R almost as far as the head of the combe, then cross it to climb the final slopes to the south-west which lead to the guide-post on Greenup. Thereafter follow Route 109 for Harrison Stickle.

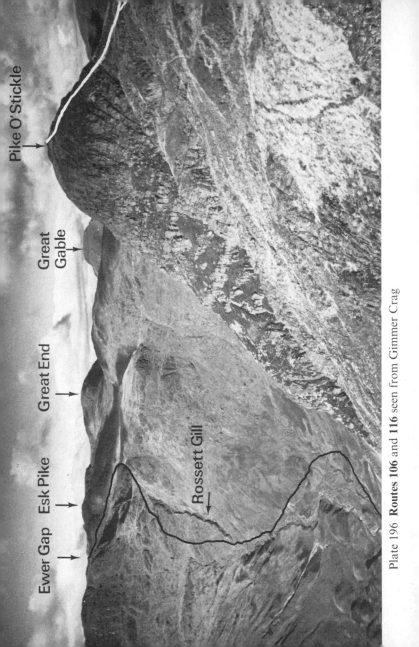

Plate 196 **Routes 106** and **116** seen from Gimmer Crag

Labels on image: Pike O'Stickle, Great Gable, Great End, Esk Pike, Ewer Gap, Rossett Gill

Plate 197 **Route 109**—Looking across the Moraine Heaps to the Lining Crag

Great Gable →   Pillar →   Glaramara →   High Stile →   Honister Crag →

Plate 198 **Route 109** — North-western prospect from High White Stones

Route 112. Grasmere and Far Easedale. Leave the Green at Grasmere by the lane going north-west between a studio on L and a white cottage on R. When the road bifurcates at Goody Bridge, take the right branch for Easedale House, which is situated at the foot of Helm Crag. Go through a gate and follow the stony track to L towards the stream, crossing it a mile farther on at Stythwaite Steps. The wild head of Far Easedale is now disclosed to the west and the track is adhered to as far as the col on the skyline. This depression is often mistaken for Greenup and is confusing in mist, because the stream beyond it is not Greenup Gill but descends through the Wythburn Valley to Thirlmere. Leave it, therefore, on R and advance along a sketchy track which rises gradually to the low ridge a mile ahead. On approaching the depression in the skyline, the Greenup guide-post will be perceived, when turn to L and follow Route 109 for the Langdale Pikes.

Route 113. by Easedale Tarn. Leave Grasmere by Route 112 but cross Goody Bridge to follow Easedale Beck which takes an almost direct line for the prominent white cascades of Sour Milk Gill. These are the key to Easedale Tarn, which lies in a great basin above them, dominated by Tarn Crag. Ascend the stony track to the dismantled refreshment hut above its outflow and continue ahead to the wild combe which may be identified by the crags of Blea Rigg high up on the L. Many parts of this section are often wet and boggy, but they may be avoided by crossing the stepping stones at the Tarn's outflow and keeping to the path on its other side. The two merge below the zig-zags and higher up pass to the L of the shapely Belles Knott which reveals a beautiful retrospect of the blue sheet of water below. Codale Tarn soon appears on the R, and on attaining the crest of the ridge ahead Stickle Tarn will be observed down on L together with the cairn of Sergeant Man higher up the hillside to the north-west. Walk up to it and thereafter cross the moorland plateau for High White Stones to join Route 109 for Harrison Stickle.

Tarn Crag →

Plate 199 **Route 113**—Paths on either side of Easedale Tarn

Langdale Pikes

Sergeant Man

Plate 200 **Route 113** passes this way

Route 114. by Silver How. Leave Grasmere by the drive to Allen Bank, but when approaching the house diverge to R along a cart road which rises to the farms of Score Crag. Leave these below on R and follow the stony track to a second gate giving access to the open fell. Pass the plantation on L and then climb southwards for the grassy top of Silver How which rises ahead. The cairn on this eminence reveals the route to the west in the direction of the Langdale Pikes, but there is no clearly defined path. Proceed to the north-west and traverse Yew Crags, then keep to the crest of the grassy hills rising to the north of Great Langdale and make for Tarn Crag, the eminence above Stickle Tarn. On attaining this top, the tarn is disclosed below; descend to its outflow and follow Route 104 to Harrison Stickle. The chief attractions of this ascent are the vista to the east over both Grasmere and Rydal, together with the splendid prospect of the hills to the west round the head of Great Langdale.

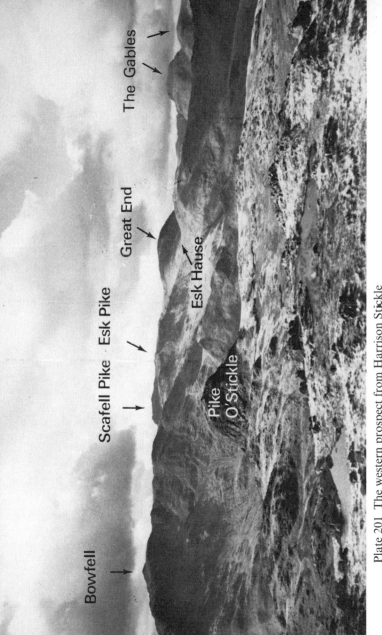

Plate 201 The western prospect from Harrison Stickle

The Bowfell group

Bowfell	2,960 feet	902 metres
Esk Pike	2,903 feet	885 metres
Crinkle Crags	2,816 feet	858 metres
Shelter Crags	2,631 feet	802 metres
Pike o' Blisco	2,304 feet	702 metres
Cold Pike	2,259 feet	689 metres

Bowfell

Route 115. Esk Hause and Esk Pike. Esk Pike rises almost due
south of the shelter on Esk Hause and the route to its summit
is unmistakable in clear weather. Leave the descending
Langdale path on L and the ascending Scafell Pike track on R,
climbing the rough slopes of the hill until the cairn is reached.
Note the precipitous front of Ill Crag on R above the head of
Upper Eskdale, and the stygian surface of Angle Tarn down
on L backed by the green strath of Mickleden far below. The
long high ridge rising to Bowfell is disclosed to the south, but
to reach it you must first descend the rough slopes to Ewer
Gap and then follow its crest to the summit, keeping well on L
above the precipices for the views down into Langdale.

The panorama from Bowfell is very fine but does not live
up to the expectations engendered by its shapely cone as seen
from below. Skiddaw and Blencathra stand in splendid
isolation on the northern horizon and the former is especially
striking when observed under snow. It rises above Glaramara,
which, however, obscures Derwentwater. The stony wastes of
the Crinkles lie to the south with the Coniston Fells
overtopping them. Pike o' Blisco looks most graceful on L
with Esthwaite and Windermere in the far distance. The green
pastures at the foot of Harter Fell are revealed on their right,
with the light glittering on Devoke Water away to the south-

west. The Langdale Pikes are disappointing to the east and are backed by the Helvellyn-Fairfield ranges. The Scafell massif rises to the west beyond the vast solitudes of Upper Eskdale, but this view of the group is not so fine as that from Long Top a mile to the south. Great Gable is in line with Great End while the Grasmoor range provides a ruddy skyline on their right.

Route 116. Rossett Gill and Ewer Gap. Follow Route 107 to the sheepfold at the end of Mickleden and take the path on L which rises in the bed of Rossett Gill. This is one of the hardest ascents in the district, and if the gradient is too steep it may be reduced by following the path which diverges to L about half-way up. On reaching the top of the gill, Angle Tarn is revealed in a rocky basin ahead with Hanging Knott on L and Rossett Crag on R. Keep to the Esk Hause path, but after passing the tarn bear to L up the cairned track for Ewer Gap and join Route 115 for Bowfell.

Map 13
The Bowfell group
Routes 115 to 127

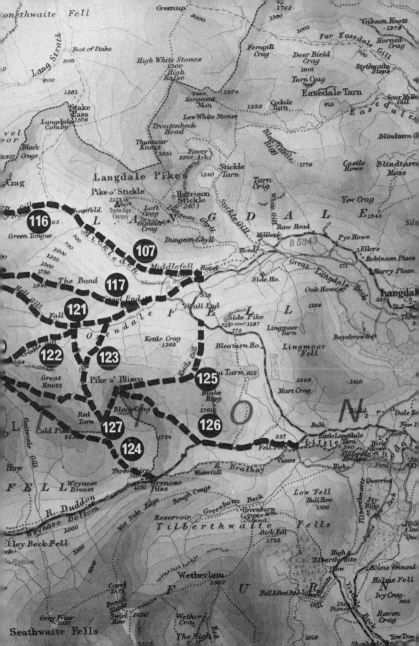

Route 117. by the Band direct. Pass through the gate at the end of the highway opposite the Old Dungeon Ghyll Hotel and follow the cart road to Stool End. Climbers who come by car may drive to a field adjacent to the farm and there park their vehicle. Go through the farmstead where a gate on L leads to the open fell. Scale the track rising straight ahead along the crest of the Band, and after crossing the marshy ground at its top climb the ridge immediately in front which rises to Bowfell. Note the fine outcrop of rock known as Bowfell Buttress on R, and on approaching the summit of the reigning peak diverge slightly to R to view the strange formation of gigantic slabs known as Bowfell Flats.

Route 118. by the Band and Three Tarns. Follow Route 117 as far as the marshy ground above the Band and then bear to L for the dip in the skyline. This discloses the pools known as the Three Tarns some little distance ahead, then turn sharp to R and climb the steep path which on reaching easier ground bears to L for the summit of Bowfell.

Route 119. Brotherilkeld and Lingcove Beck. Follow Route 6 to the packhorse bridge over Lingcove Beck. Do not cross it, but take the less distinct track on R of this tributary stream and keep to it as far as Green Hole, which lies immediately below and to the west of Three Tarns. Make your way up the steep slopes on R beside a beck where Bowfell towers overhead on L. On reaching the stony wilderness, go ahead to Three Tarns and pick up Route 118 for the summit of the mountain.

Plate 202 **Routes 117** and **118** are clearly revealed from Side Pike

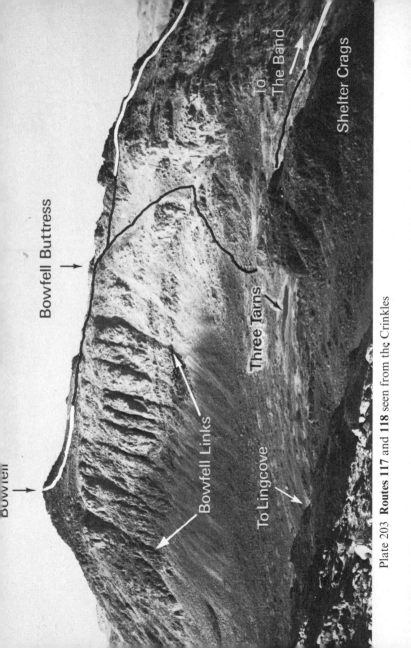

Bowfell

Bowfell Buttress

Bowfell Links

Three Tarns

To Lingcove

To The Band

Shelter Crags

Plate 203 **Routes 117** and **118** seen from the Crinkles

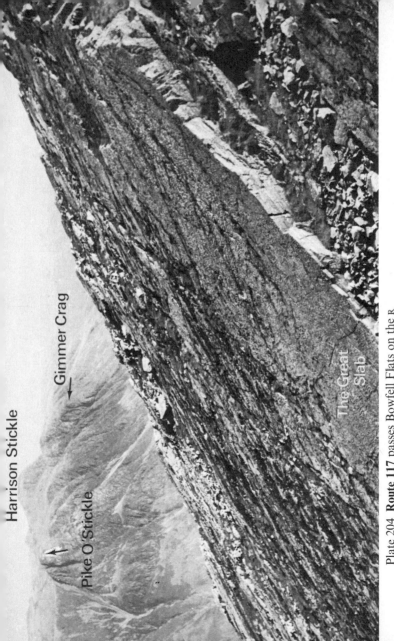

Harrison Stickle

Gimmer Crag

Pike O'Stickle

The Great Slab

Plate 204 **Route 117** passes Bowfell Flats on the R

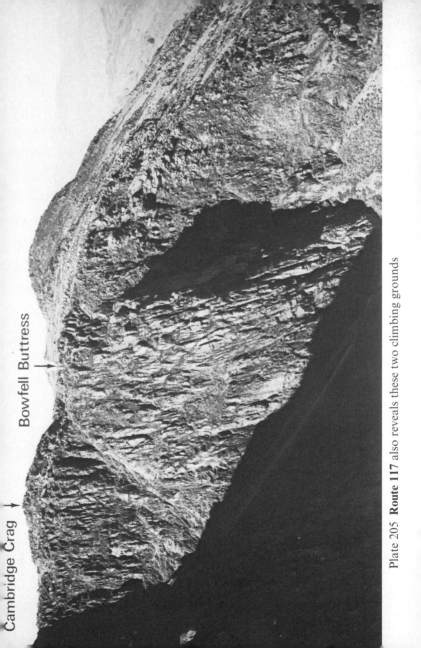

Cambridge Crag

Bowfell Buttress

Plate 205 **Route 117** also reveals these two climbing grounds

Scafell   Mickledore   Scafell Pike   Ill Crag

Three Tarns

Plate 206 **Route 118** passes Three Tarns

Plate 207 **Route 119** from Harter Fell

Crinkle Crags

Route 120. From Three Tarns. Proceed due south from the three pools and make your way through the maze of Shelter Crags as a prelude to the traverse of the more lofty ridge of the Crinkles. Keep well on L near the edge overlooking Langdale to scan the many rifts on its eastern front, and to observe with delight the winding course of the great valley at your feet. Note especially the impressive Mickle Door on L immediately below Long Top, for it discloses an attractive aspect of Pike o' Blisco across Browney Gill far below, and is the exit usually climbed by those who have ascended Crinkle Gill. There are two conspicuous features in the panorama from Long Top which are worthy of special mention. The prospect of the Lakeland Giants is most revealing, for the two Scafells are clearly delineated to the north-west, and particularly so the topography of the more westerly peak. The rift enclosing Cam Sprout is well seen, as also the depression above it which terminates with Mickledore. In addition to this spectacle of wild mountain grandeur, Bowfell discloses its real majesty to the north with Skiddaw peeping over its right shoulder. Moreover the gullies of rotten rock known as Bowfell Links are clearly perceived seaming its southern façade high above one of the greatest stony wildernesses in Lakeland.

Route 121. by Hell Gill. Follow Route 117 to Stool End. Go through the farmstead where a gate on the L leads to the open Fell. Pass the track to the Band on the R and walk to a prominent stile L over the first wall and then descend to the beck in Oxendale. Pass the sheepfold on the R to another stile over its wall whence the track becomes very stony and later decked with boulders galore. Here great care is necessary until the bridge over Hell Gill is reached.

Now cross the footbridge whence there are two variations beside Hell Gill. The more popular ascends a steep grassy spur and on reaching higher ground it bears R and keeps to the edge of the wild ravine. The other follows the beck to Whorneyside Force, crosses the stream below it and then climbs with the gill on L. Both eventually continue ahead over grass to the col on the skyline, and on reaching Three Tarns turn sharp L and follow Route 120 for Crinkle Crags.

Route 122. by Crinkle Gill. Follow Route 121 as far as the footbridge; cross it and walk L to the wild rocky exit of Crinkle Gill but enter it only when the stream is not in spate. Thread an impressive rocky canyon to emerge in a deeply enclosed basin where several streamlets come together. Climb the shattered crags on R to escape from it and then follow the main beck to its source. The two rocky bastions of Mickle Door now tower overhead; keep them on R until the gully splitting them is disclosed. Scramble up its scree bed to gain the skyline and then turn L for the highest Crinkle and later R to set foot on Long Top. A quicker but less interesting alternative that is, however, very steep and arduous starts up the track to Hell Gill. After attaining the top of the first rise it takes a direct line for the highest Crinkle, first over grass and then through scattered boulders to the base of the long stone shoot which slants R up to the skyline. The ascent of this section is hard going but some of it can be avoided by bearing L up steep and rugged slopes until the L branch of the stone shoot is encountered. The last 200 feet of it cannot be avoided and it emerges on the skyline just to the R of Mickle Door.

Windermere

Pike O'Blisco

Mickle Door

Plate 208 **Route 120** opens up a fine view of Pike o' Blisco

Plate 209 Crinkle Crags—**Routes 121, 122** and **123** and variations

Shelter Crag

Plate 210 **Route 121** passes the fall of Whorneyside Force

Plate 211 **Route 121** goes up either side of Hell Gill

To Cold Pike

To Red Tarn

Great Knott

Crinkle Gill

Browney Gill

Highest Crinkle   Mickle Door

Pike O Blisco

Plate 212 **Routes 122, 123** and **124** to Crinkle Crags

Route 123. by Browney Gill. This stream is deeply enclosed on both sides and the tracks keep well away from it until its higher reaches are attained. The most direct route is to follow Route 121 to the sheepfold and to then ford the stream hereabouts. On the other side pick up the track that slants diagonally uphill to a depression well up the flanks of Pike o'Blisco and continue high above Browney Gill R until Red Tarn appears ahead. Do not go round it, but cross the stream near its outflow and then take an oblique course across the lower slopes of Cold Pike, keeping a wild ravine on R. On reaching easier ground make for the skyline to the west, whence bear R for the highest Crinkle and Long Top. During the latter part of the ascent there are magnificent views R into the savage recesses of Crinkle Gill, and later on there is a Bad Step below the first top which, however, may be turned on L. A circuitous but less steep variation goes round the base of the spur of Pike o' Blisco and later merges with the first route.

An alternative is to follow Route 121 to the footbridge over Hell Gill. Cross it and bear L to ascend the grassy ridge with Browney Gill on L. It reaches the skyline L of Great Knott and later passes behind this eminence to join Route 123 between Cold Pike and the Crinkles. At the beginning of this variation there is a less distinct track that forks R; it makes for the cascading stream R of Great Knott and on attaining higher ground skirts the rim of Crinkle Gill and goes direct to the dominating Crinkle. This is a sporting course but the going is steep and rough until the plateau is reached.

Route 124. Wrynose and Cold Pike. Take the track going in a north-westerly direction from the Three Shire Stone at the top of Wrynose Pass, and keep straight ahead for Cold Pike which is the southern sentinel of the Crinkles. Then proceed in a north-westerly direction along the crest of the broad grassy ridge to pick up Route 123 for Long Top and the Crinkles.

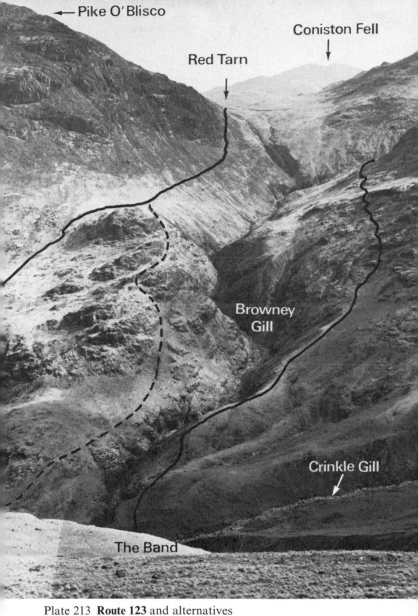

Plate 213 **Route 123** and alternatives

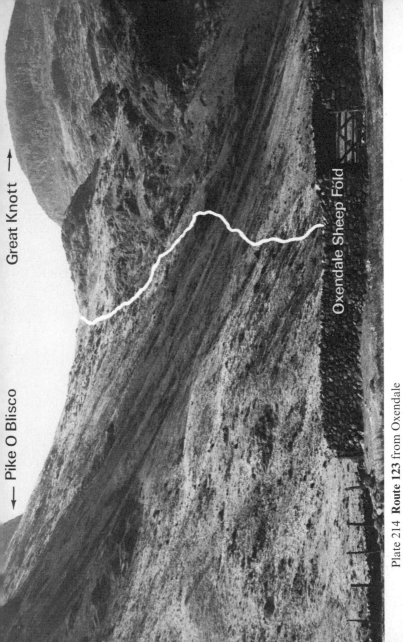

← Pike O Blisco

Great Knott →

Oxendale Sheep Fold

Plate 214 **Route 123** from Oxendale

Cold Pike

Track To Crinkle Crags

Browney Gill

Red Tarn

Plate 215 **Route 123** is very popular with fell walkers

Scafell Pike

Scafell

Mickledore

Long Top

Cam Spout Crag

Upper Eskdale

Plate 216 The Lakeland Giants from the Crinkles

Pike o' Blisco

Route 125. Langdale and Kettle Gill. Leave the terminus of the highway opposite the Old Dungeon Ghyll Hotel, and walk along the road to the farm of Wall End. Go through a gate on L and follow its steep and sinuous course which ultimately leads to Little Langdale by way of Blea Tarn. Before reaching the second gate desert the road for the open fell and ascend a path through the bracken which contours across the slopes on R. Pick up Kettle Gill and follow the main stream to its source, keeping the outcrop of Kettle Crag well on R. Then bear due west and climb the final slopes of Pike o' Blisco. This peak was formerly crowned by the most beautiful cairn in Lakeland and commands a grand prospect of Great Langdale, as well as one of the most impressive aspects of the shattered front of Crinkle Crags.

Route 126. Little Langdale and Fell Foot. Fell Foot is the last farm in Little Langdale and stands at the bottom of Wrynose Pass just short of its junction with the road going over to Blea Tarn and Great Langdale. Ascend the pass as far as the bridge spanning the stream coming down from Pike o' Blisco, and then turn off to R beyond it to pick up the track which rises to the summit of this mountain.

Route 127. From Red Tarn. Ascend Route 123 as far as Red Tarn and then turn sharp to L up the fellside, following the small cairns to the summit of Pike o' Blisco.

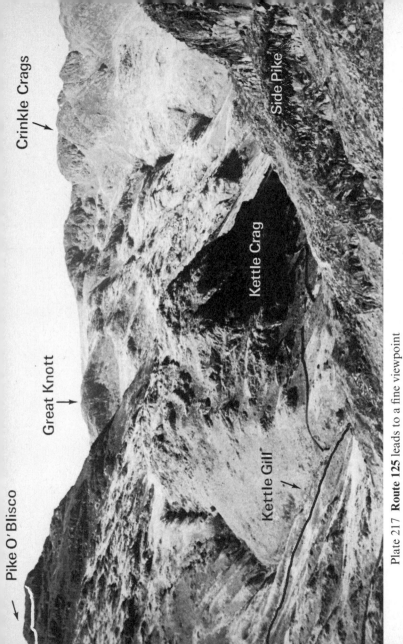

Pike O' Blisco

Crinkle Crags

Great Knott

Side Pike

Kettle Crag

Kettle Gill

Plate 217 **Route 125** leads to a fine viewpoint

Fairfield

St.Sunday Crag

Helvellyn

New Dungeon Gill Hotel

Old Dungeon Ghyll Hotel

Pike O'Blisco

Plate 218   North-east from Pike o' Blisco

The Coniston group, Harter Fell and Border End

Old Man	2,631 feet	802 metres
Swirl How	2,630 feet	802 metres
Brim Fell	2,611 feet	796 metres
Carrs	2,575 feet	785 metres
Dow Crag	2,555 feet	779 metres
Grey Friar	2,537 feet	773 metres
Wetherlam	2,502 feet	763 metres
Brown Pike	2,239 feet	682 metres
Walna Scar	2,035 feet	620 metres
Harter Fell	2,143 feet	653 metres
Border End	1,703 feet	519 metres

Coniston Old Man

Route 128. by the Quarries. This is the shortest, least
interesting but most popular ascent of the mountain. Leave
Coniston by the turning on L of the Sun Hotel and follow the
track across a field and over a footbridge when Church Beck
appears on the R. Ascend beside the beck, but on reaching the
open fell do not cross the bridge to the disused Copper Mines.
Instead, pass through a gap in the wall on the L and follow
the upper path that sweeps round the hillside, when the
summit of the Old Man is revealed to the west. Advance
towards it and drop down slightly to the quarry road coming
in on the L from Fell Gate, which follow to the workings
below Low Water. When the track forks take the R branch
which ultimately discloses the tarn in a wild setting. Skirt its
south side and climb the zig-zags which rise to the ridge
leading to the R for the cairn on the summit of the mountain.

    This route may be varied by taking the uphill lane on R just
short of the bridge in the village. It passes through a gate and
swings round to L to join Church Beck, whence the previous

Plate 219 Dow Crag and Coniston Old Man from Torver

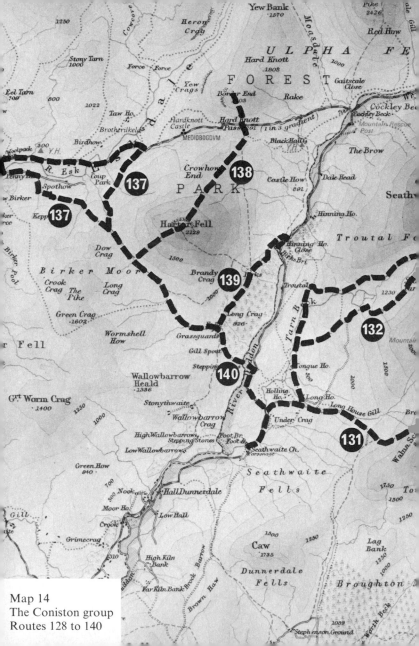

Map 14
The Coniston group
Routes 128 to 140

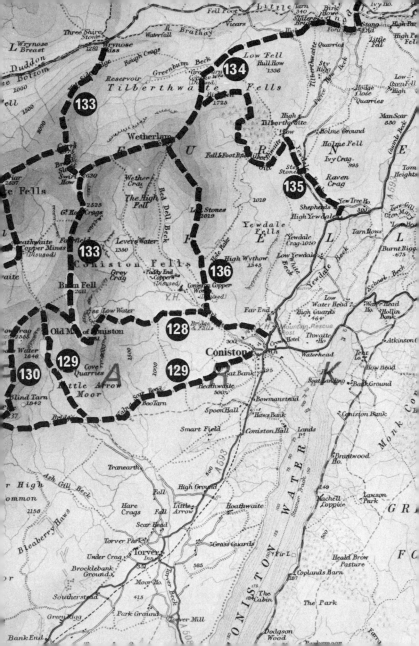

route may be reached by crossing the bridge near the falls. Alternatively, the stream may be kept on L as far as the Youth Hostel, whence a track goes to L and ascends the slopes of the Old Man to join the first route near Low Water.

The panorama from the Old Man is famous for its extensive prospects to the south and east, where the patterned fields and wooded knolls stretch away to the sea in the dim distance. The most conspicuous feature in this vast landscape is Coniston Lake, which is revealed completely far below. There are also glimpses of Tarn Hows and sections of Windermere to the east, while the sands of the Duddon gleam far away in the south-west to L of the great whaleback of Black Combe. The view round the rest of the arc contrasts strangely with this sylvan scene, for it reveals a confused mass of mountains without disclosing a single peak in its entirety. The summit of Dow Crag lies to the west, but to see Goats Water at its base it is necessary to descend some distance below the cairn. The Central Fells appear to the north-west above the rounded top of Grey Friar, while Skiddaw, Saddleback and the Helvellyn range rise above Brim Fell and Wetherlam to the north. The long line of hills dominated by High Street are seen to the north-east and terminate in the south with the columnar beacon of Thornthwaite Crag and the graceful cone of Ill Bell.

Route 129. by Goats Water. Leave Coniston by the lane rising to the old railway station, but pass under the bridge and ascend the steep road ahead. This climbs up to Fell Gate and then bends to R for the quarries on the eastern face of the Old Man. Take the grassy Walna Scar Road on its left which undulates over the open fell at the base of the reigning peak, passes the reedy pool known as Boo Tarn, and then rises through three rock gateways with Brown Pike dominating the skyline to the west. After passing the last gateway turn sharp to R across the moor and follow the grassy track to a prominent quartz cairn, whence the stony path is seen bending to L to enter the wild combe at the base of Dow

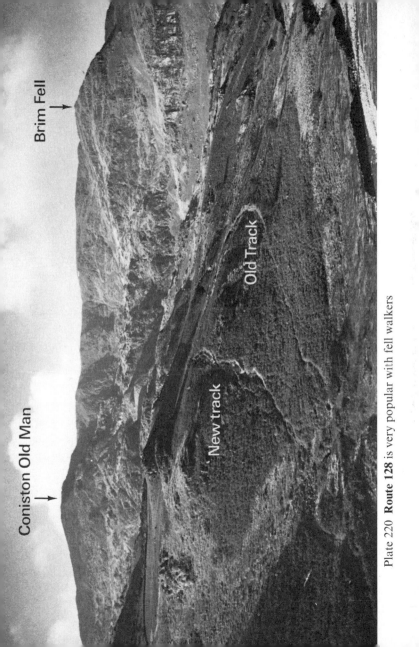

Plate 220 **Route 128** is very popular with fell walkers

Crag. On rounding the escarpment on R, Goats Water appears immediately ahead. Keep it on L and make for the dip in the skyline to the north. On attaining the grassy col, bear sharp to R for the cairn on the Old Man. During the latter part of the ascent the five magnificent rock buttresses of Dow Crag frown upon the vast scree slopes and the black waters of the tarn at their base. They are one of the most important climbing grounds in Lakeland and beloved by the expert cragsman.

Plate 221   **Route 128**—Looking down on Low Water and the Quarry track from Coniston Old Man

Plate 222 The vast north-western prospect from the summit of the Old Man

Walna Scar Road →

Plate 223 **Route 129**—Boo Tarn is often passed unseen

Dow Crag

Goats Water

Track to Goats Water

Quartz Cairn

Plate 224 **Route 129**—Dow Crag is first unveiled from this cairn

Plate 225 **Route 129**—Dow Crag from Goats Water

Route 130. Walna Scar and Brown Pike. Follow Route 129 to the third rock gateway on the Walna Scar Road. Continue along it in the direction of Brown Pike, passing over Cove Beck bridge which reveals the zig-zags up the slopes of Walna Scar to the west; climb them until the col is attained. On reaching the cairn the view bursting on the eye to the west is one of the surprises of this route, for it discloses not only the Duddon Valley below but also the long line of hills stretching from Black Combe on L, over the vast solitudes of Birker Moor in front, to the shapely peak of Harter Fell on R. The Scafell Pikes rise on the northern horizon and sweep round to Bowfell, which peeps over the western flanks of Brown Pike in the foreground. Now turn sharp to R and ascend the grassy slopes of this eminence, whose cairn reveals a fine prospect to the east and south which is not dissimilar to that seen from the Old Man. Walk northwards along the crest of the broad ridge to Buck Pike, noting the perfect circle of Blind Tarn below on R, and on reaching the latter cairn observe the splendour of the view which encompasses the Lakeland Giants, Dow Crag and Coniston Old Man on the other side of Goats Water, far below. Now walk along the ridge and ascend the final slopes of Dow Crag, meanwhile noting the great yawning gullies on R which form the savage recesses of this magnificent crag. Climb carefully over its cairnless summit and while descending the rough rocky ridge to Goats Hause note the fine conical form of Harter Fell on L. Here join Route 129 for the summit of Coniston Old Man.

Route 131. Seathwaite and Walna Scar. Leave the hamlet by the Cockley Beck road going north through Dunnerdale and keep Tarn Beck on L until the bridge spanning it appears ahead. Here the road forks; take the right branch which bends round to R and follow it past Long House with Long House Gill on L. This bifurcates again when the left branch rises to Seathwaite Reservoir, but take the stony track on R which goes up the fellside to the east. Leave some unsightly quarry workings on R and gain the grassy track which bends

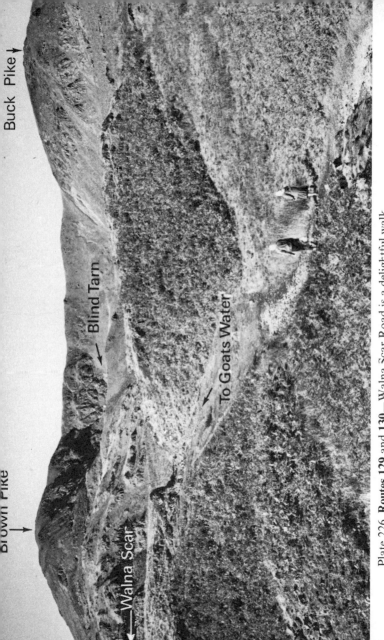

Buck Pike →

Blind Tarn →

Brown Pike ↓

← Walna Scar

To Goats Water →

Plate 226 **Routes 129** and **130**— Walna Scar Road is a delightful walk

round to L and rises across the flanks of Walna Scar. Turn to R for the col, and on reaching the cairn ascend Brown Pike on L and follow Route 130 for Dow Crag and the Old Man.

Route 132. Seathwaite and Grey Friar. Take Route 131 as far as Long House. Go through the farmstead and follow the cart road to Tongue House half a mile to the north. Follow Tarn Beck for a short distance but turn to R at the first streamlet entering it, and scale the side of the hill until the dam of Seathwaite Reservoir comes into view ahead. This point may be reached by the gated road beyond Long House but the walk is not so pleasant. Pass round the eastern shore of the reservoir and at its head cross the stream to attack the final slopes of Grey Friar to the north. A more direct route keeps Tarn Beck on L for over a mile beyond Tongue House, and after crossing the main stream rises in a north-easterly direction over the craggy knolls of Troutal Fell to the cairn on Grey Friar. The prospect to the north-west from this outpost of the Coniston Fells is incredibly beautiful and one of the most impressive in Lakeland. The fine serrated skyline of the Scafell group rises above the wild recesses of Upper Eskdale, and the eye is irresistibly led towards them over the wastes of Mosedale far below, between the craggy, hummocked top of Hard Knott on L and the declivities of Stonesty Pike on R. Cockley Beck and Wrynose Bottom are hidden by the slopes of Grey Friar in the foreground, but the symmetrical cone of Harter Fell is well seen in isolation to the west. Now turn your steps eastwards and descend to the broad col with its prominent cairn, then swing round to R above Seathwaite Reservoir and make for Great How Crags in the south-east. This top overlooks Levers Water with Coniston and its lake far below, and also discloses the long whaleback ridge of Brim Fell to the south which terminates with the Old Man. Walk along its many undulations to attain the cairn on the reigning peak.

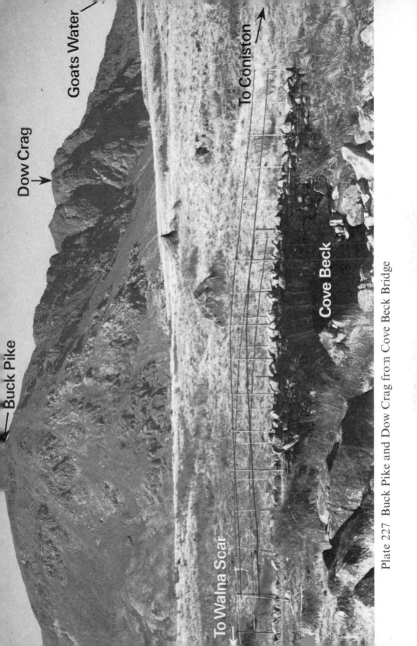

Plate 227 Buck Pike and Dow Crag from Cove Beck Bridge

Brown Pike

Blind Tarn

Plate 228 **Route 130** is the only walk that reveals Blind Tarn

Plate 229 An interesting section of **Route 130**

Plate 230 **Route 130** yields a close view of the precipices of Dow Crag

Plate 231 **Route 132** opens up a spacious prospect from the Walna Scar Road

Plate 232 **Route 132**—The Scafell Pikes from Grey Friar

Swirl How

Route 133. Wrynose, Carrs and Swirl How. Leave the Three
Shire Stone on Wrynose, cross the road and ascend the steep
grass by a track which leads to a small cairn on the horizon.
This discloses the large key cairn on Wet Side Edge as shown
in plate 234, whence bear R and continue along the well worn
path to Carrs which is the highest northern sentinel of the
range. Energetic fell walkers may prefer to keep to the edge of
the precipices on the L, surmounting the several craggy
satellites en route. The cairn discloses a wide panorama of fell
and dale with Pike o' Blisco to the north and the Crinkles on
its left. These are overtopped by Bowfell, which merges with
the Scafells in the north-west, while the Helvellyn range rises
on the north-eastern horizon well above the intervening
moorland. The most attractive vista, however, is to the east,
where Greenburn Tarn is cradled in the vast combe far below,
with the light reflected by Little Langdale Tarn beyond it, and
the Fairfield range forming a great barrier across the skyline
in the background. Walk southwards round the shattered rim
of Broad Slack and climb to the cairn on Swirl How, then
continue in the same direction along the ridge to Great How
Crags and Brim Fell for the Old Man of Coniston. Those
coming from Fell Foot may follow the River Brathay for
some distance and then ascend Wet Side Edge direct.

Plate 233 **Route 133** reveals the length of Wet Side Edge

Plate 234—**Route 133**—The key cairn on Wet Side Edge

Carrs

Swirl How

Prison Band

Carrs

Helvellyn

Griesdale Hause

Fairfield

Hart Crag

Green Burn
Tarn

Plate 235 **Route 133**—Green Burn Tarn from Carrs

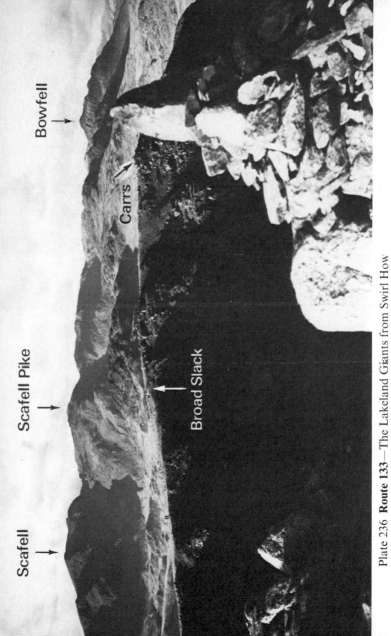

Plate 236 **Route 133**—The Lakeland Giants from Swirl How

Wetherlam

Route 134. Little Langdale and Wetherlam. Take the left fork
at the post office in the village and go downhill by the road
leading to the ford across the River Brathay. Walk over the
footbridge and turn to R by the stream, leaving the tarn on R
and following the cart road to High Farm. Climb the walled
road beyond it, and on emerging on the open fell cross the
Tilberthwaite cart road and bear to L over the lower slopes of
Hull How. There is no track, but a way will be found on the
right of Birk Fell which leads to a marshy col overlooking
Tilberthwaite Gill to the south. Climb over a fence and ascend
the craggy flanks of Wetherlam to the south-west until the
cairn on its summit is attained. The view round the northern
arc is superb and includes the Scafells, the Crinkles and
Bowfell, the Langdale Pikes and the Helvellyn range. The
Pikes, however, present a disappointing aspect owing to their
lower elevation and appear much more impressive from the
ridge lower down in the vicinity of Birk Fell. The vista to the
east also is magnificent, for it reveals the flatter green country
towards Windermere and includes the head of Coniston Lake,
Tarn Hows and Esthwaite as well as a section of this lake.
Descend westwards from the summit for about a mile until
the col is reached immediately below Swirl How, noting
Levers Water down on the left. Scramble up the rocky ridge
of Prison Band to this top and follow Route 132 which
undulates to the left to finally reach the summit of the Old
Man.

Coniston Old Man Lad Stones Wetherlam Carrs Wet Side Edge Wrynose Pass

Little Langdale

Skelwith Bridge

Plate 237 **Route 134** as seen from Langdale

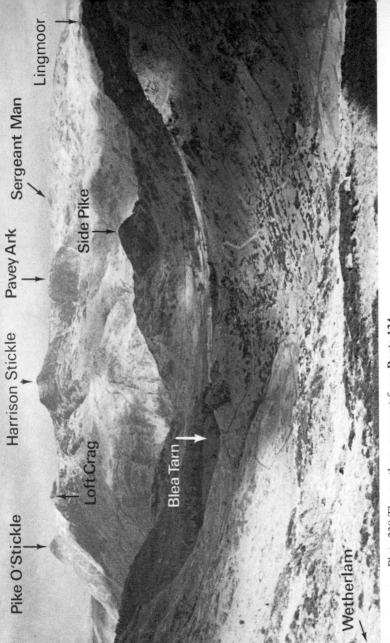

Pike O'Stickle

Loft Crag

Harrison Stickle

Pavey Ark

Sergeant Man

Lingmoor

Side Pike

Blea Tarn

Wetherlam

Plate 238 The northern prospect from **Route 134**

Birk Fell

Wetherlam

Lad Stones

Hole Rake

Tilberthwaite→

Plate 239 **Routes 135** and **136**—Wetherlam and Yewdale

Route 135. Tilberthwaite Gill and Wetherlam. This wild and picturesque ravine is one of the favourite venues of the Lakeland visitor, but since the ladders and wooden bridges were swept away in a storm the watercourse can no longer be followed, save by the adventurous climber. At the time of writing two of the bridges in the lower recesses of the ravine had been rebuilt, but as the higher one ended in a wall of rock the course terminated at this point. However, the exit of the ravine may be reached by ascending either side of it as follows: 1. Park the car in the old slate quarry beside the bridge spanning the gill and ascend the track on L. On reaching the old quarry road turn R and when it bifurcates take the L branch which reveals grand views of the gill low down on R. This path eventually crosses the gill on level ground and turns R to join the original path on the open fell. 2. Cross the bridge from the car park and go through a gate on R of stream. Follow the grassy path to a stile over a wire fence on L, and at this point scale the rough ground on R, passing through scanty trees to reach the other quarry road above. Walk along this gradually rising course, with the gill low down on L, until it merges with the path on the open fell. Wetherlam now towers overhead, but the easiest approach is by the rough track on R which ends below and to the south of Birk Fell. The quarries are passed on L and the ridge above them ascended to join Route 134 for the summit of the mountain.

Route 136. Coniston and Wetherlam. Leave the village by Route 128 but cross the bridge to the disused copper mines. Follow it for a few yards and then take the grassy cart track on the R which rises gently across the hillside to Hole Rake. Cross the stream and bear L by an indistinct track for the ridge leading to Lad Stones. Proceed over its many tops until the cairn on Wetherlam is attained, noting the fine views on the L of Great How Crags, Swirl How and Carrs. Then follow Route 134 for the summit of the reigning peak. This is the easiest ascent, but a variation may be made by bearing L along a track half way up the hillside and when well above Red Dell Beck turning R for the steep climb to Lad Stones. A steeper alternative is to leave the village by the uphill road on L, just short of the bridge over Church Beck. Desert it some short distance beyond the gate and ascend the slopes of High Wythow. Traverse the many ups and downs of this eminence until the small tarn of Hole Rake appears below and then proceed as detailed above.

Plate 240 **Route 135**—Tilberthwaite Gill and its bridges

Swirl How

Wetherlam

Plate 241 **Route 136**—Coppermines Valley

High Wythow

Fairfield

Lad Stones &
Wetherlam

Plate 242 **Route 136** passes across Hole Rake

Carrs

Swirl How

Great How Crags

Plate 243 **Route 136**— Western prospect from Lad Stones

Plate 244   **Routes 135** and **136**—Pike o' Stickle from the summit of Wetherlam

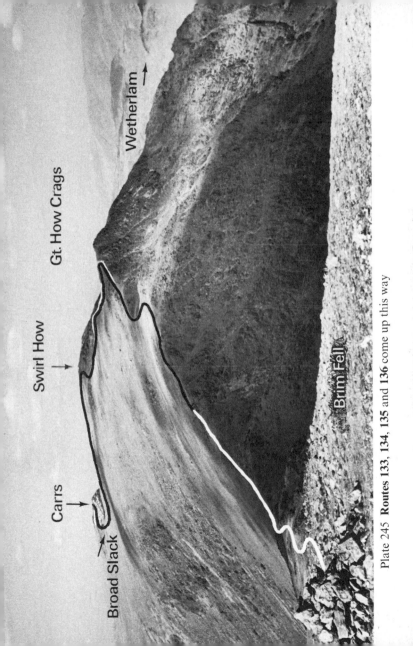

Carrs → Broad Slack

Swirl How ↓ Gt. How Crags

Wetherlam ↑

Brim Fell

Plate 245 **Routes 133, 134, 135** and **136** come up this way

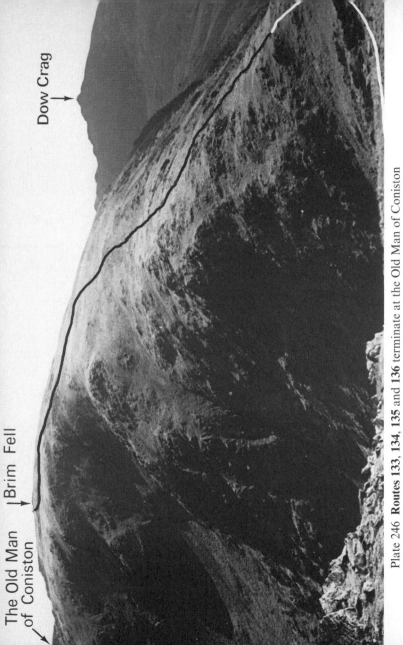

The Old Man
of Coniston

Brim Fell

Dow Crag

Plate 246 **Routes 133, 134, 135** and **136** terminate at the Old Man of Coniston

Harter Fell

Route 137. Eskdale and Penny Hill. Leave the Eskdale
highway by the road on R just short of the Woolpack Inn.
Cross Doctor Bridge which spans the River Esk and turn to L
through a gate to follow the farm road to Penny Hill. Pass
through the farmstead and bear R along a grassy cart road
which rises gently to a gate in a wall. Pass through the gate
and follow the L branch of this grassy cart road until a
dilapidated branch wall appears ahead. Scramble over it and
keep to the main wall on L until a corner is reached, then turn
sharp L and follow it as it contours almost level across the
craggy hillside for about half a mile. On reaching a cairn,
where the wall now goes L down the fellside, continue to
contour below the crags on R. Cross a stream, beyond which
the track bifurcates. The L branch is your route, as the R
branch ascends through the crags and is the way to
Grassguards and Dunnerdale. Thence the path is confusing as
it winds its way in and out below the crags until a deep ravine
enclosing the turbulent Spothow Gill is encountered. Make
your way across it and climb its steep eastern bank to a wall
on L which follow to a gate through which passes the track
from the foot of Hardknott Pass. Thereafter your route is
clear as it rises across the open fell and skirts the collection of
massive crags on L before attaining the three conspicuous
rocky cones that crown the summit of the mountain. These
afford some easy scrambling and their tops cannot be reached
without the use of the hands. This route is the most
interesting and revealing ascent of Harter Fell, because as
height is gained all the Lakeland Giants appear one by one on
L across Eskdale, whereas the clearer variation, often referred
to as the main route which starts from the cattle grid on
Hardknott Pass, has all the views behind the climber, with the
only compensation of the vista along Eskdale on the R. The
splendid isolation of the summit of Harter Fell opens up a
panorama in all directions and includes the green straths of
both Eskdale and Dunnerdale together with the massive

group of hills dominated by the Old Man of Coniston. It is the vista to the north, however, that will hold your gaze, for the Scafells rise superbly above Upper Eskdale and form a magnificent skyline which merges on R with Bowfell and the Crinkles, while the thin line of the road rising to Hard Knott Pass threads the valley at your feet.

Route 138. From Hard Knott Pass. Proceed southwards from the crest of the pass and make your own route to the summit of Harter Fell, traversing the innumerable grassy hummocks with fine views of Dunnerdale and Wrynose Bottom on L, and of Eskdale on R backed by Muncaster Fell and the Irish Sea.

Note—Border End is the rocky northern extremity of Hard Knott and unveils the most dramatic view of the Lakeland Giants, from Scafell to Bowfell. To attain it all you have to do is to climb about 500 feet from the crest of Hard Knott Pass and walk north. This diversion is one of the most repaying in all Lakeland. See plate 3.

Route 139. From Birks Bridge. Owing to the rapid growth of the extensive plantations on the eastern flanks of Harter Fell, which now reach the 1,500 feet contour, it is easier to follow the cart track to Birks Farm and continue along it to Grassguards, whence bear R until the plantations end. Then turn sharp R and ascend over rough grass to the summit of Harter Fell, avoiding the craggy outcrops throughout the climb.

Route 140. Seathwaite and Grassguards. Follow Route 131 to the bridge over Tarn Beck, cross it and keep to the road until it rounds a craggy knoll on R. Then take a path on L which drops down the slopes to Fiddle Steps, cross them and climb the track to Grassguards, keeping the stream on L all the way. Pass the farmstead near a bridge and take the Eskdale track, but leave it in half a mile to make for the summit of Harter Fell, due north and on R.

Plate 247 Harter Fell is reached by **Routes 137, 138** and variations

Labels on image: Grassguards, Penny Hill, Harter Fell, Hardknott Pass, Coup Park, Wha House

Plate 248 **Route 137**—The rocky summit of Harter Fell

To
Harter Fell

Plate 249 **Route 139**—Birks Bridge. The pools below are
a favourite with bathers

Grassguards   Harter Fell   Birks Bridge

To Cockley Beck

To Seathwaite

Plate 250   **Route 140**—The prospect of Harter Fell from Dunnerdale

This **Route Card** is now in use in Scotland and Snowdonia; the idea is sound and if adopted and used consistently by all climbers and walkers throughout our mountainous country it could be the means of facilitating any call for Mountain Rescue. It is, of course, most important that **no digression** is made from the stated route, otherwise in the event of an accident searchers would be unable to locate the victim.

Leave word
when you go
on our hills

Names and Addresses: Home Address and Local Address	Route
Time and date of departure	Bad weather alternative
Place of Departure and registered number of vehicle (if any)	
Estimated time of return	Walking/Climbing (delete as necessary)

GO UP WELL EQUIPPED — TO COME BACK SAFELY

Please tick items carried

Emergency Food	Torch	Ice Axe
Waterproof Clothing	Whistle	Crampons
(colour:	Map	Polybag
Winter Clothing	Compass	First Aid
(colour:		

Please complete and leave with landlady, warden etc.
Ask landlady or warden to contact Police if you are overdue
<u>PLEASE REPORT YOUR SAFE RETURN</u>

An Appeal from Mountain Rescue Teams

FELL WALKERS! READ THIS

and live a little longer...

British mountains can be killers if proper care is not taken. The following notes cover the <u>minimum</u> precautions if you want to avoid getting hurt or lost, and so inconveniencing or endangering others as well as yourselves.

CLOTHING. This should be colourful, warm, windproof and waterproof. Wear boots with nails or moulded rubber soles, <u>not</u> shoes, plimsolls, or gum-boots. Take a woollen cap and a spare jersey; it is always colder on the tops.

FOOD. <u>In addition to</u> the usual sandwiches take chocolate, dates, mint cake or similar sweet things which restore energy quickly. If you don't need them yourself, someone else may.

EQUIPMENT. This <u>must</u> include map, compass, and at least one reliable watch in the party. A whistle and torch (a series of six blasts or flashes repeated at minute intervals signal an emergency) and, in winter conditions, an ice-axe and survival bag are <u>essential.</u>

COMPANY. Don't go alone, and make sure party leaders are experienced. Take special care of the youngest and weakest in dangerous places.

EMERGENCIES. Don't press on if conditions are against you — turn back even if it upsets your plan. Learn a little first aid, and keep injured or exhausted people warm until help reaches you. Get a message to the Police for help as soon as possible, and report changes of route or time-table to them if someone is expecting you. The Police will do the rest.

This is a copy of the leaflet published and distributed free of charge by the Lake District Mountain Accidents Association, with the help of voluntary donations from the public.

DANGERS WHICH CAN ALWAYS BE AVOIDED—
and should be, until you know how to cope with
them:

Precipices
    Slopes of ice,
        or steep snow,
            or very steep grass (especially frozen),
                or unstable boulders.
Gullies and stream beds.
    Streams in spate.
        Snow cornices on ridges or gully tops.
            Over-ambition.
                Plain damned carelessness.

DANGERS WHICH MAY SURPRISE YOU—
and should be guarded against:

Weather changes -- mist, gale, rain or snow.
  Get forecasts, and watch the sky.

Ice on paths.
  Carry an ice-axe.

Excessive cold or heat.
  Dress sensibly, and take a spare jersey.

Incipient exhaustion.
  Know the signs; rest and keep warm.

Accident or illness.
  **Don't panic. If you send for help, make sure that
the rescuers know exactly where to come.**

Flight of time.
  Learn your own pace. Plan your walk.

It is no disgrace to turn back if you are not certain.
A party must be governed by the capabilities of the
weakest member.

THINGS TO THINK OF BEFORE YOU SET OUT

Can you use map and compass in mist or storm?
(Be prepared before you're caught).

Do you know the safe ways off in emergency? (If the map
doesn't tell you, ask someone who does know.)

How will you keep the party together? (Stragglers may
mean trouble and danger to yourselves and others.)

Who knows where you are going and when you should be
back? (If you come down somewhere else, send word at
once, or get in touch with the Police.)

ENJOY YOURSELVES, BUT DON'T PLAY THE FOOL

Index

Aaron Slack, 119
Accident Procedure, 61
Adam Seat, 334
Alcock Tarn, 290
Allen Crags, 148
Ambleside, 286
Angle Tarn, 309

Band, the, 366
Bannerdale, 309
Base Brown, 117
Bassenthwaite, 250
Beck Head, 112, 132
Belles Knott, 357
Bessyboot, 142
Birkhouse Moor, 268
Birkness Combe, 190
Birks Bridge, 428
Black Beck Tarn, 200
Black Combe, 400
Black Sail, 132
Blake Rigg, 238
Bleaberry Tarn, 184
Blea Rigg, 357
Blea Tarn, 340
Blea Water, 318
Blencathra, 246, 253
Blind Tarn, 401, 404
Boardale Hause, 309
Boo Tarn, 392
Border End, 41, 388, 428
Borrowdale, 23
Bowfell, 362
Brackenclose, 100
Braithwaite, 224
Brandreth, 114
Breast Track, 119
Brim Fell, 402, 426
Broad Crag, 76
Broad Slack, 409
Broad Stand, 86
Brocken Spectre, 61
Brotherilkeld, 80, 366

Brothers' Water, 296, 299
Brown Pike, 400
Brown Tongue, 66, 86
Browney Gill, 380
Buckbarrow, 335
Buck Pike, 403
Burnmoor, 94
Buttermere, 181, 215

Caiston Glen, 299
Cam Crag, 142
Cam Spout, 84, 92
Cam Spout Crag, 94
Carl side, 250
Carrs, 409
Castlerigg, 253
Castle Crag, 222
Catbells, 222
Catchedicam, 268, 284
Causey Pike, 232
Chapel Stile, 336
Climbers' Traverse, 124
Climbing Equipment, 13
Clothing, 16
Cockley Beck, 400
Codale Tarn, 357
Cofa Pike, 291, 295
Cold Pike, 380
Coledale Pass, 228
Comb Door, 142
Comb Gill, 140, 142
Comb Head, 142
Coniston, 388
Coniston Old Man, 388
Coniston Fells, 388
Corridor Route, 76
Crinkle Crags, 373
Crinkle Gill, 374, 380
Crummock Water, 181

Dale Head, 204
Daw Crags, 228
Deepdale, 296

Deepdale Hause, 291
Derwentwater, 221
Distance and Times, 58
Distress Signal, 61
Dock Tarn, 352
Doddick Fell, 254
Dollywagon Pike, 274
Dore Head, 166, 178
Dove Crag, 296
Dovedale, 296
Doves Nest Caves, 140
Dow Crag, 392, 399, 406
Druid's Circle, 256
Duddon River, 392
Dungeon Ghyll, 336, 346
Dunnerdale, 400

Eagle Crag, 148
Easedale, 357
Easedale Tarn, 357
Eel Crags, 210
Ellas Crag, 232
Elterwater, 340
Ennerdale, 112, 171
Equipment, 13
Erosion, 340, 343, 346
Eskdale, 427
Esk Falls, 80, 92
Esk Hause, 76, 96
Esk Pike, 362
Esthwaite Water, 340
Ewer Gap, 340, 362

Fairfield, 286
Far Easedale, 357
Fell Foot, 385
Fell Walking, 434
Fisher Gill, 283
Fleetwith Pike, 196
Floutern Tarn, 203
Froswick, 328

Garburn Pass, 328
Gaskell Gill, 242
Gate Scarth Pass, 331
Gatesgarth, 192
Gavel Neese, 104, 112
Gillercombe, 116

Gillerthwaite, 169, 203
Gimmer Crag, 346
Glaramara, 138
Glenderaterra, 260
Glenridding, 265
Glories, 61
Goats Water, 392, 399
Gore-Tex, 18
Grain Gill, 148
Grange, 222
Grasmere, 277, 290, 357
Grasmoor, 224
Grassguards, 427, 428
Great Door, 178
Great Doup, 154
Great End, 96
Great Gable, 45, 104
Great How Crags, 409
Great Knott, 380
Great Langdale, 340
Great Rigg, 290
Green Gable, 114
Greenhead Gill, 291
Greenhow End, 296
Greenside Mines, 283
Greenup, 352
Grey Friar, 402
Grisedale, 268, 274
Grisedale Pass, 274
Grisedale Pike, 224, 231
Grisedale Tarn, 274, 277, 291

Hall's Fell Top, 253
Hanging Knott, 363
Hardknott Pass, 427, 428
Harrison Stickle, 336
Hart Crag, 296
Harter Fell, Eskdale, 388, 427
Harter Fell, Mardale, 324, 331
Hartsop Hall, 296
Hartsop above How, 296
Haweswater, 314, 320
Haycock, 169
Hayeswater, 309
Haystacks, 196
Heights of Lakes and Tarns, 35

Heights of Passes, 34
Heights of Peaks, 32
Hell Gill, 373, 378
Helm Crag, 357
Helvellyn, 265
Heron Pike, 290
High Crag, 190
High House Tarns, 150
High Knott, 142
High Level Route, 151
High Raise, 352
High Scarth Crag, 84, 94
High Stile, 181
High Street, 302
High White Stones, 352
Hindscarth, 219
Hobcarton Crags, 228, 242
Hole Rake, 418, 422
Hollowstones, 92
Honister, 114, 137, 213
Howtown, 312
Hunsett Cove, 296

Ill Bell, 324
Innominate Tarn, 201

Jacks Rake, 340
Jaws of Borrowdale, 250
Jenkin Hill, 246

Kentmere, 318, 324
Keppel Cove, 285
Kern Knots, 125
Keswick, 222, 260
Kettle Gill, 385
Kidsty Pike, 316
Kinn, 224
Kirkfell, 132
Kirkstone Pass, 299
Knitting How, 222

Lad Stones, 417, 423
Lakes, Heights of, 35
Langdale, 340
Langdale Pikes, 336
Langstrath, 148
Lanthwaite, 242
Lanty's Tarn, 265

Latrigg, 246
Levers Water, 402
Lingcove Beck, 366
Lingmell, 100
Lingmell Gill, 100
Lining Crag, 352
Link Cove, 296
Little Hart Crag, 286
Little Langdale, 385, 414
Lobstone Band, 204
Loft Crag, 346
Long Sleddale, 331
Long Top, 363, 373
Looking Stead, 151
Lord's Rake, 86
Loweswater, 228
Low Hartsop, 302
Low Water, 388

Maiden Moor, 206
Mardale, 314
Measand Beck, 314
Mellbreak, 181
Mickleden, 350, 363
Mickledore, 66, 84
Mickle Door, 374
Millbeck, 250
Mill Gill, 336
Mireside, 265
Mosedale, 166
Moses's Trod, 137
Moses's Sledgate, 137
Mountain Accidents
    Association, 434
Mountains, Heights of, 32
Mountain Photography, 37
Mousthwaite Comb, 253
Mungrisdale, 253

Nab Scar, 290
Nailing, 14
Nan Bield, 318, 331
Napes Needle, 127
Napes Ridges, 126
Netherbeck, 168
Newlands, 215
Nine Becks Walk, 169

Old Man of Coniston, 388
Overbeck, 166, 178
Oxendale, 373

Pasture Beck, 302
Passes, Heights of, 32
Patterdale, 265, 268
Pavey Ark, 336, 340
Peaks, Heights of, 32
Penny Hill, 427
Photography, 37, 50
Piers Gill, 71
Pike o' Blisco, 350, 385
Pike o' Stickle, 336
Pillar Fell, 151
Pillar Rock, 159, 163
Place Fell, 286
Prison Band, 414

Rainsbarrow, Crag, 325
Raise, 283
Rake Gill, 80
Rampsgill Head, 312
Raven Crag, 302
Rakes Progress, 87
Red Pike, 166, 203
Red Screes, 299
Red Tarn, 270, 380
Riggindale, 312
River Brathay, 409
River Glenderamachin, 253
River Greta, 260
Robinson, 151, 215
Rock Climbing, 21
Roman Road, 322
Rossett Crag, 363
Rossett Gill, 351, 363
Rosthwaite, 138, 204, 350
Rosthwaite Cam, 142
Rosthwaite Fell, 142
Rough Crag, 318
Routes, Notes on, 26, 57
Route Finding in Mist, 60
Rowling End, 234
Ruddy Beck, 184
Ruthwaite Cove, 274
Rydal, 286

Saddleback, 246
Sad Gill, 331
Sail, 232
Sail Beck, 238
St. Sunday Crag, 291
Sand Hill, 228
Satura Crag, 309
Scafell, 86
Scafell Pike, 66
Scale Force, 181
Scales, 253
Scandale Pass, 286, 299
Scar Crags, 232
Scarth Gap, 192
Scawdel Fell, 218, 222
Scoat Fell, 169
Scoat Tarn, 168
Scope End, 218
Screes, 62
Seathwaite, Borrowdale, 119
Seathwaite, Dunnerdale, 400,
    428
Seatoller, 116
Seat Sandal, 277
Sergeant Man, 357
Shamrock, 151, 160
Sharp Edge, 253
Shelter Crags, 377
Silver How, 360
Skew Gill, 96
Skiddaw, 246
Slab & Notch, 161
Sleet Hause, 234
Slight Side, 94
Small Water, 318
Sour Milk Gill, Borrowdale,
    116
Sour Milk Gill, Buttermere,
    186
Sour Milk Gill, Easedale, 345
Sphinx Ridge, 104
Sphinx Rock, 129
Sprinkling Tarn, 196
Stair, 232
Stake Pass, 350
Stanger Gill, 142
Stangs, The, 296
Starling Dodd, 203

Steeple, 171, 173
Stickle Barn, 25
Stickle Tarn, 336
Sticks Pass, 283
Stirrup Crag, 178
Stockley Bridge, 120
Stone Arthur, 290
Stonethwaite, 142
Stoney Tarn, 94
Stool End, 366
Striding Edge, 270, 275
Sty Head, 71, 119, 124
Stythwaite Steps, 357
Sweden Bridge, 286
Swirral Edge, 268
Swirl How, 409

Tarn at Leaves, 142
Tarn Hows, 392
Tarn Crag, 357
Tarns, Heights of, 35
Taw House, 84, 94
Taylor Gill, 119
Thirlmere, 353
Thirlspot, 277
Thornhow End, 291
Thornthwaite Crag, 302, 328
Thornythwaite Fell, 138
Three Shire Stone, 380, 409
Three Tarns, 366
Threlkeld, 254
Thresthwaite Cove, 302

Tilberthwaite, 414, 418
Troutbeck, 324, 328

Ullscarf, 352
Ullswater, 292

Wall End, 385
Walna Scar, 392, 400
Wandope, 238
Wansfell, 299
Warnscale Bottom, 196
Wasdale, 22, 62
Wastwater, 49, 108
Weather Hill, 312
Westmorland Cairn, 111
Wetherlam, 414
Wet Side Edge, 409
Whin Ben, 242
Whinlatter Pass, 224
Whiteless Pike, 239
Whiteside, 242
White Side, 277
Whorneyside Force, 374
Windermere, 287, 337
Wind Gap, 166, 171
Windy Gap, 112
Woolpack Inn, 94, 427
Wrynose, 380, 409
Wythburn, 277, 353

Yewbarrow, 178
Yoke, 324